The Librarian's
Introduction to
Programming Languages

Library Information Technology Association (LITA) Guides

Marta Mestrovic Deyrup, Ph.D., Acquisitions Editor,
Library Information and Technology Association,
a Division of the American Library Association

The Library Information Technology Association (LITA) Guides provide information and guidance on topics related to cutting-edge technology for library and IT specialists.

Written by top professionals in the field of technology, the guides are sought after by librarians wishing to learn a new skill or to become current in today's best practices.

Each book in the series has been overseen editorially since conception by LITA and reviewed by LITA members with special expertise in the specialty area of the book.

Established in 1966, the Library and Information Technology Association is the division of the American Library Association (ALA) that provides its members and the library and information science community as a whole with a forum for discussion, an environment for learning, and a program for actions on the design, development, and implementation of automated and technological systems in the library and information science field.

Approximately twenty-five LITA Guides were published by Neal-Schuman and ALA between 2007 and 2015. Rowman & Littlefield took over publication of the series beginning in late 2015. Books in the series published by Rowman & Littlefield are:

Digitizing Flat Media: Principles and Practices
The Librarian's Introduction to Programming Languages

The Librarian's Introduction to Programming Languages

A LITA Guide

Edited by Beth Thomsett-Scott

ROWMAN & LITTLEFIELD
Lanham • Boulder • New York • London

Published by Rowman & Littlefield
A wholly owned subsidiary of The Rowman & Littlefield Publishing Group, Inc.
4501 Forbes Boulevard, Suite 200, Lanham, Maryland 20706
www.rowman.com

Unit A, Whitacre Mews, 26-34 Stannary Street, London SE11 4AB

British Library Cataloguing in Publication Information Available

Library of Congress Cataloging-in-Publication Data Available

ISBN 978-1-4422-6332-1 (cloth : alk. paper)
ISBN 978-1-4422-6333-8 (pbk : alk. paper)
ISBN 978-1-4422-6334-5 (ebook)

∞™ The paper used in this publication meets the minimum requirements of
American National Standard for Information Sciences—Permanence of Paper
for Printed Library Materials, ANSI/NISO Z39.48-1992.

Printed in the United States of America

The Librarian's Introduction to Programming Languages is dedicated to all librarians seeking to take up programming and who feel that they don't have the basics to begin. It is my hope that this book will fill that void.

I also dedicate it to Carol Scott, my amazing daughter,
who perseveres through the highs and lows of life,
and David Scott, my best friend through the travels this world gives us.

Peace to all.

Contents

Illustrations

FIGURES

TABLES

EXAMPLES

Acknowledgments

This book came to be through some circuitous events. The original editor needed to withdraw, and Marta Deyrup, editor for the LITA Guide series, put me in touch with Ron T. Brown, and we agreed to work as coeditors. After the original concept for the book was approved, Ron was offered a job in industry and accepted it. This new position kept Ron too busy to work further on the book. By this time, a few chapter authors had other commitments and I needed to recruit replacements. There was also a bit of delay while moving from a previous publisher to Rowman & Littlefield.

With the above said to set the stage, I want to offer my grateful thanks to Marta Deyrup for her confidence in me, Ron for guiding the concept of the book, and all my original authors who have hung in there for nearly two years. Many additional thanks to the amazing authors who stepped in at the near last minute to provide excellent chapters.

Preface

A Librarian's Introduction to Programming Languages provides an overview of the most popular programming languages used in libraries, including practical examples that will help librarians get past the "I can't do it" stage. We start with Python, Ruby, and JavaScript, which are considered the most readable and thus relatively easier-to-learn languages, which also have numerous applications. Perl, PHP, and SQL follow, as they are a bit trickier but incredibly useful. C, C#, and Java complete the book as compiled languages, with their own ins and outs, yet they have a number of important uses in libraries.

While there are books and websites devoted to teaching programming, few works address multiple programming languages or provide library-specific examples. The audience for this book is composed of administrators, practitioners, students, educators, and other lifelong learners interested in computer programming.

This book is designed to provide a basic working knowledge of each language presented, examples where the language is used in libraries, ideas of when a librarian would find each language useful, and small examples for practical experience. Recommended resources are provided for additional reading. The contributed-chapter format allows a wider spectrum of languages to be covered from a greater variety of experiences.

On behalf of the contributors, I wish all readers the very best of luck in creating new programs for their personal and professional use or consulting with programmers to implement a new or redesigned technology. We offer our sincere hope that these chapters guide you to a lifelong enjoyment of programming regardless of your current level of skill and knowledge. Happy programming!

Chapter One

Introduction

Dean Walton

HISTORY AND DEVELOPMENT

Programming has come a long way from its beginnings to today. My first introduction to programming was using punch tape, the same tape that was used to deliver changing stock market prices. For those familiar with the classic 1960s sitcom *The Adams Family*, Gomez was always pouring over his ticker tape. The next major developments were punch cards and Fortran (http://www.fortran.com/). With the advent of the personal computer, programming became accessible as a pastime for the masses. Programming is especially interesting since, in some cases, programmers may not even want or have to use a computer. A programmer can write a script on a piece of paper, comprehend the flow of logic, and never need to see it actually run. Programming is effectively the documentation of logic to solve a task. It can be a game, a puzzle to solve, just like the morning crossword. However, other people want to get a task done and use the computer to do it.

Computers are now integral to the work of librarians, and because many computer programs allow users to customize and run short program segments, called scripts, librarians could be missing out on a huge slice of the library world if they do not learn a few programming basics. As an example, if you have budget data, you can perform repetitive analyses to calculate various scenarios. With circulation data, you can perform repetitive analyses to examine use of items by certain populations, call number range use related to semesters, and other important relationships. Programming allows a person to perform complex repetitive tasks quickly and allows for quick modification as parameters change.

So how does a librarian with no programming experience start? First, let's understand that the terms *program* and *program code* are fairly interchangeable. A program is a complete set of stand-alone program code. Program code typically refers to code in general, not a complete program. Programming is the action of creating a program, essentially writing the code that makes up a program. Code is the English-like instructions we humans use to tell a computer what to do. You may have heard of programmers or coders. These are essentially the same thing: people who write (or code) programs. One might say that learning to program is now kids' play. There are a plethora of books, online videos, and game-oriented websites that can help. One of these, Code .org, is a great site for basic instruction; it teaches the logic of programming regardless of the programming language. Code.org provides tutorials and content for elementary kids to learn the building blocks of programming. Of course, adults can learn from the site as well and do it in fun ways. If you want something more advanced, then YouTube is just a click away with its wealth of step-by-step videos. One must be careful, though, to ensure the quality of the instruction. The resources provided by chapter authors and the Additional Resources section of this book will guide you to quality items for your trek through the land of programming.

THE BASICS

It is important to make a distinction between interfacing with a computer and programming on it. A first step for many adults, including librarians, is to practice interfacing skills. A good way to start is to pull out an old desktop or laptop computer and load Linux on it. The newest versions of Ubuntu Linux, an operating system, will, when loaded, resemble Windows or Apple OS. However, in Linux, it is still possible to have a mouse-driven graphical user interface and enter the "Terminal" (X-terminal), where running the computer is command driven. By this I mean that the user can type commands on the appropriate lines on the computer, hence the name "command line." Gone is the mouse and its cursor. To move around the computer, the user uses the arrow keys. On a Windows machine, you can hold down the Windows key (often at the bottom left of the keyboard) while also holding down the X key. This brings up a menu for the command line and also the command line with administrator rights.

There are several important tasks to learn in the command line. In order to function in this environment, the user must learn how to move back and forth between different folders or directories; move, copy, or delete contents within these folders or directories; and find, download, and unpack programs from other sources. Mastering this suite of tasks will serve the librarian very well.

Once these are achieved, loading the sets of scripts, or libraries, needed for a particular programming language will be much easier.

The starting point for all of this is the path (figure 1.1). This is what allows the user to know where everything resides in the file structure of the operating system. The path follows terminology that is analogous to a tree. The structure that connects a tree to the earth and the trunk to the tree are the roots. The very core of the path is the *root directory*. The root structure contains the commands that allow the computer to function. Any deletion of files in the root and the computer won't work; thus the root directory is often protected. Protection in this case means needing a password to change parts of the root directory. If you are the administrator for the computer, that is, it's your computer or you are responsible for it, then you should know the root password. Creation of the root password normally happens when you load the operating system onto your computer.

The user can add or delete folders from the root directly just as a tree can grow new branches or a gardener can trim them away. But, remember, if you cut out the roots, the tree will die. A good question is how you know what branches your tree pathway has. You can type *dir* in the command line and

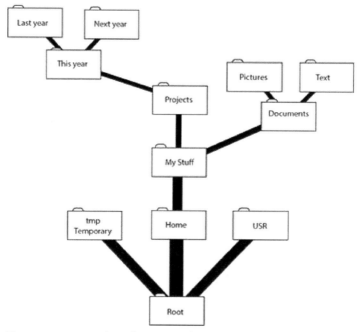

Figure 1.1.   A generic path structure for folders or directories in a computer operating system.

see a list of folders contained within your location. To move into one of those folders, you type *cd*, short for "change directory," and the directory's name. There is even an easier way to go back to where you just were. By typing a single period on the command line and hitting enter, you ask the computer to bring you back to the previous folder. If you type two periods, you ask the computer to take you back to the starting point of all of the directories, back to the root directory.

There are also some added functions to many of these commands. A good example is how you can view the contents of a folder in Windows. You can view contents as a list or a list with details regarding size and creation date. The new user will be confronted with terms like *tar*, *grep*, and *bash*. Some of these refer to concepts that are easy to understand for someone used to Windows or Mac OS. For example, a .tar file is one that is compressed, like a zipped Windows folder. It needs to be uncompressed and the files contained within the folder moved to the appropriate folders or directories to be useful. Certain files need to be placed in an existing folder while others need to be placed in a brand-new folder that the user may need to create. It is important to read any associated text file or instructions on how to unpack and set up the new program.

It is likewise important to learn that Linux is designed to run some tasks without question while asking about others. This keeps the user from accidentally trashing the contents of the computer. In many Linux systems, this is defined as the *SUDO* user or super user. All that is really happening is that the operating system is asking the user to authenticate that she or he is the administrator of the computer and that the changes are actually desired. This helps to keep unauthorized users from making changes. In Linux, the user has the ability to peer into the operating system and pretty much make any changes that he or she requests, regardless of whether or not the change will stop the computer from functioning. This means the administrator has a lot of power, and a lot more power to mess up things than users of Windows have over their machines.

Once the user has Linux running on a computer and has decided which of the really cool programs to load for free, the next step is loading or downloading the packages for the language of your choice. The author has learned bits and pieces of programming based on what he wanted to do. In order to load and run the program BibApp, he had to learn the basics of a language called Ruby, but he didn't need to learn everything about Ruby. This is where learning a spoken language differs a great deal from learning a computer language. For program users, often only the very basics are needed to get a whole series of very different programs up and running. Actual programming, well, that is a different matter. Having a task always makes learning to program easier.

An example of a simple and fun programming challenge is something along the lines of a Sumo robot competition. In this venue, two small robots set with motion detectors and line sensors compete to push each other out of a three-foot circular ring. These robots have motors to drive two wheels and when turned on and placed in the playing field, the robots seek each other out and try to push each other out of the ring. The programmer needs to write a script commanding the robot to do what and when, based on it detecting the other robot. The programming can be fairly simple, and it is a way to look at applied programming problems—and robotics. Again, the logic for defining the tasks would likely be the same for any computer language, just expressed differently.

GETTING STARTED

Today, buying a project book for an Arduino, Raspberry Pi, Edison, or BeagleBone (http://beagleboard.org/bone) and the matching computer board for twenty to eighty dollars is a great way to have fun and learn programming at the same time. These are all types of microcontrollers. A few are advanced and perform more like current computers. A microcontroller is a set of programmable switches that you tell the controller to turn on and off as needed and for as long as desired. You can turn on lights, motors, or power sensors and collect and save data. With any of these, you can make intriguing projects, such as a wall-mounted electronic calendar that updates itself as a person updates his or her own personal calendar (Chee 2014) or your own robot.

Most programs can be written in a text editor, such as NotePad if you are a Windows user. A program like Word won't work because it will add a lot of hidden text material not visible to the writer, which will keep the program from working. In contrast, NotePad doesn't add this material. However, not all text editors are the same, and some are much more useful than others. Some text editors can add color-coding to different parts of the program. Sublime Text and NotePad++ are two widely regarded and utilized editors, with the former working on Windows and Linux operating systems. Each provides the user with numbered lines to track sections of the program.

Almost any new user will be confronted with a type of "Hello World" script. Whether a person is working in Perl or in Python, most tutorials start here. The student defines a variable, such as X = "Hello World." The next step is just to command the computer to show the variable on the screen (Print X). The end result is that the student will see "Hello World" on his or her computer screen.

As more and more programs become open source, meaning that the programming script (code) is publicly available, the power of programming for the librarian grows. A great example of this is with the program R. R is a statistical package. It is written and modified by users around the world, who continually add to and improve it. If there is a task you want the program to do and there is no script to run the task, you can write the script and then use other functions of the program to, for example, graph the results. Once you have written your script, you can share it with others so that they can benefit from your work. Along the way, someone else will probably bundle your script with a series of other related scripts and it will be added as a library to the program. The same is true for a program like QGIS, an advanced mapping program that can perform complex spatial analysis. Users can write short programs that provide much greater function to the overall QGIS program.

OBJECT-ORIENTED PROGRAMMING

This brings us to the concept of object-oriented programming. Object-oriented programming is the process of writing scripts or short programs that can be plugged into or cut out of larger programs without causing any failures to either the larger program or the script in the process. With object-oriented programming, you can write a script to perform a task. This script is the object. Others can use your object (script) and plug it into an entirely different program to perform the same task you wrote it for on your program. For example, you could write a script to take some sort of sensor data, say book counter data from an automated check-in conveyor belt, and then aggregate the data daily and provide the weekly average of books that are turned in to the library. Another person could then copy your script to use with a different sensor to provide the weekly average number of patrons going through the library door. The task of creating the weekly average is the same whether you are counting books or people. It is this kind of chunked programming that has led to the development of very powerful programs and allowed the person on the street to add to it. The goal is to avoid having to rewrite the whole program just because you want to add one new task (to learn more, visit *PC magazine*'s definition at http://www.pcmag.com/encyclopedia/term/48238/object-oriented-programming).

A fun way to begin programming is to work on puzzles where the reader is asked to solve a task by writing a script. Anyone can search online for examples of these. There are also books on programming puzzles. However, some of these books contain complex puzzles, and it seems these puzzles are used in the interview process when firms hire new programmers. For beginners, don't shy away from books written for kids. Jason Briggs's *Python for*

Kids is a great starting point, and his website (http://jasonrbriggs.com/python-for-kids/puzzles.html) posts simple programming challenges for beginners.

In any event, one of the easiest ways for a beginner to learn programming is by having fun working on projects where failure is a learning experience and not a security or function problem. Again, Arduino projects are great for this type of activity. My best suggestion is to load Linux (it's free) on an old laptop, buy an Arduino for twenty dollars, and spend some time on the web with Code.org.

PROGRAMMING IN LIBRARIES

Finally, why should a librarian learn to program? To collect data and solve problems such as how many books within the call numbers range $x–y$ were checked out more than once in any given year over the last ten years, to determine if checkouts are related to student success, to examine the effectiveness of library instruction—and many other reasons.

This brings us to deciding which language to learn. Generally, this is going to depend on the reason behind wanting to learn. If the goal is a specific task, the language choice will be affected. For many librarians, writing the most concise code is probably less important than writing code that others can easily interpret. This is why languages such as Ruby and Python are popular. They are fairly concise, but more importantly, a person reading the script can easily see what the script is trying to do.

A recent report in the *Communications of the Association for Computing Machinery* (Guo 2014) indicated that Python was the most popular language of 2014. This was based on an analysis of recent classes taught in university computer science departments and indicates that many programs are now written in Python. Thus it will probably be one of the best languages to start with unless there are reasons to use something else. Python is simple and powerful, and you will able to write interesting scripts fairly easily. If you are mainly involved in web design, then Java may be a better fit. There is no need to learn too many languages. Once you learn one language and have a good grasp of basic programming terminology and concepts, it will be easier to pick up another language when needed or desired.

In 2015, Stephen Cass of the Institute of Electrical and Electronics Engineers published a list of what he considered the most important programming languages of the last year (Cass 2015). Most of the languages listed can also serve any librarian interested in programming, but probably not in the same order of importance. The list also comes close to matching the content of this book. The list is reordered below for the benefit of a librarian-oriented audience and based on the author's personal communications with programmers. Definitions for these and other computer programming language can be found at the site maintained by Bill Kinnersley at Kansas University, called *The Language List* (http://people.ku.edu/~nkinners/LangList/Extras/langlist.htm).

Python—An easy-to-interpret object-oriented language and therefore quite popular.

Ruby—A very easy programming language to interpret. Ruby on Rails provides a way to use Ruby with a set of protocols and structure to create responsive and dynamic websites.

PHP—A language that allows the calling of data from a web server so that is it visible in a web browser. It is one of the main tools for suppling web-based information, such as the content of a store's merchandise catalog.

Java—A server-oriented language that is also object oriented and that can run on multiple platforms or computer types. It shares some similar syntax to C and C++. Its ability to run on different operating systems makes it a useful language.

Perl—One of the most widely used object-oriented programming languages. There is very good support for the language. Its main competitor is probably the newer Python, which has the advantage of being easier to interpret.

JavaScript—A client-based (working on your local computer) language that works in web browsers with data pulled from the web by the browser. It is what powers the functionality of web browsers. JavaScript is an important language for anyone creating web-based applications.

SQL—A language that allows for the organization and intense data mining of very large data sets.

R—A programming language that is designed for statistical analysis. This language provides for basic and advanced analysis, is flexible regarding data formats, and has associated scripts that allow for versatile data visualizations.

The remaining popular languages are quite powerful and allow a programmer to write efficient code in the fewest number of lines. Each is also worthy of learning for the intrepid or for librarians thinking of programming as their major job responsibility. However, these languages will be the hardest to interpret for a person just learning programming or who may only be programming as just a small part of her or his job: C, C++, C#, and C-Objective.

STEPS FOR LEARNING TO PROGRAM

1. Visit Code.org and start playing with programming. Anyone can start here and all that is needed is an Internet connection. However, this only gets a person's brain working on the abstract concepts of programming and doesn't provide the practical part of implementing a program.

2. Go to the Ubuntu Linux site (http://www.ubuntu.com/download) and download the latest version of Ubuntu as an ISO file. This will take some time as it is likely to be around a gigabyte in size. The ISO file is one that is bootable and that a computer will load upon start up. Now, burn this file to a DVD or to a flash drive. Windows (http://windows.microsoft.com/en-us/windows7/burn-a-cd-or-dvd-from-an-iso-file) or the open-source program 7-Zip can provide this function. 7-Zip can be downloaded from http://www.7-zip.org/download.html and can provide other important archiving functions not directly related to the task here.

3. Find an old computer (laptop or desktop) that is no longer in use and where no one cares about the contents on the hard drive. This is a critical review point. All data will be overwritten on the hard drive, so be certain that its contents are no longer important. Turn on the computer and load the ISO file into the DVD drive. Allow Ubuntu to install and to overwrite the hard drive. This step is irreversible, and the program will warn you about this. Say yes, allow the program to install, and accept the default options. Prompts for language, keyboard, and time zone will come up. Select the appropriate ones.

4. The program will ask you to create a password. Create one and write it down. As this is a training computer, the password is a formality needed to run the computer. If it is ever forgotten, you can reinstall Ubuntu with the same ISO DVD and start over.

5. With Ubuntu installed, you can go right to the terminal command line using the keyboard command Ctrl-Alt-T and start learning command line directives. The important part here is that learning how to navigate the command line in Linux will allow you to implement programs that you write.

6. Part three of this set of steps is to buy a forty-dollar Arduino starter kit from Amazon.com and download the Arduino programming package and install this on a Windows, Apple, or Linux machine. You can now start programming an Arduino unit and have it follow a program and actually see the results of the program. The starter kit, an Arduino with associated parts and manual, is the best bet over just purchasing an Arduino board without parts.

7. Start reading, writing, and practicing on Linux and the Arduino, and have fun.

The chapters in this book will help readers decide which language to begin with and to assess when to learn additional languages. The practical examples will lead you through the basics of each language. It is my hope that all readers will find their own favorite language and reach their goal of becoming fluent programmers for whatever task and whatever reason led them to purchase this book. Welcome to the world of computer programming!

BIBLIOGRAPHY

Cass, S. 2015. "The 2015 Top Ten Programming Languages." *IEEE Spectrum*, July 20. http://spectrum.ieee.org/computing/software/the-2015-top-ten-programming-languages.

Chee, Brian. 2014. "Hero Hacks: 14 Raspberry Pi Projects Primed for IT." *InfoWorld*, July 10. http://www.infoworld.com/article/2606860/consumer-electronics/158674-Hero-hacks-14-Raspberry-Pi-projects-primed-for-IT.html.

Guo, Philip. 2014. "Python Is Now the Most Popular Introductory Teaching Language at Top U.S. Universities." *Communications of the Association for Computing Machinery*, July 7. http://cacm.acm.org/blogs/blog-cacm/176450-python-is-now-the-most-popular-introductory-teaching-language-at-top-us-universities/fulltext.

Chapter Two

Python

Charles Ed Hill and Heidi Frank,
with Mark Pernotto

HISTORY AND DEVELOPMENT

Python is an open-source high-level scripting language used for a variety of purposes, from fast, small analysis programs to large-scale applications. Although it is difficult to measure how many users open-source projects have, it is estimated that Python has around a million users and is in the top five or ten most commonly used programming languages in the world (Lutz 2013). One reason for this popularity is Python's flexibility; it can support object-oriented, functional, or good old procedural, do-this-then-that programming paradigms. More important, though, are some of the explicit design features of Python that make it a language focused on code quality, developer productivity, portability between operating systems, and integration with Python tools and other languages. In other words, you can quickly write Python code that is powerful; easily readable; works unchanged on Mac OS, Windows, and Linux; and hooks in easily with a variety of tools. This design philosophy is made explicit in "The Zen of Python" by Tim Peters (2004), which includes statements like "Readability counts" and "Simple is better than complex." If you have Python installed, open a Python interpreter and type "import this," and you can read "The Zen of Python" in its entirety. These kinds of ideas make Python not only a robust, powerful language able to fit a variety of needs, but an approachable language to learn, a great first language for programming, and a great tool for sharpening library work flows.

Python was created by Guido van Rossum while working at the Dutch research institute CWI (a Dutch acronym that translates as the Center for Mathematics and Computer Science) in 1989. Twenty years later, he wrote a series of blog posts detailing its history and development (Van Rossum 2009–2013). Named after Monty Python, an association that persists in the documentation as "spam" variables and several quick quips, it was originally coded mostly over the Christmas season to serve as a side project to "bridge the gap" between C and the shell to speed up development of system administration tools. Van Rossum based many aspects of the language on ABC, a language he had recently worked as a developer on, while taking cues from C and other more obscure languages. He worked with an explicit design strategy that emphasized speed of development, ease of use, readability, borrowing from others whenever possible, and making Python easily extendable.

After initial development by Van Rossum and his colleagues, Python was released on the alt.sources newsgroup with an MIT license on February 20, 1991. With encouragement from the community, Van Rossum continued to update the language, and in 1993 the comp.lang.python newsgroup, which persists to the present day, was started. In 1994, a major topic of conversation on the list was aptly titled "If Guido Was Hit by a Bus," in which members of the community worried about the fate of the language given that Van Rossum continued to make many of the updates personally. Partially as a result of this thread, Van Rossum was invited to the United States to work with the National Institute of Standards and Technology in 1994. Amid these conversations of his hopefully-not-imminent demise and coming to America, Python 1.0 was launched, and in 1995 Van Rossum began work at the Corporation for National Research Initiatives, where several more major releases were launched. Simultaneously, during attempts to diversify Python development by forming a semi-official group to oversee development, Van Rossum was bestowed with the title of Benevolent Dictator for Life, signifying his continued last-say in all things Python (Lutz 2013).

After the Python team did a stint with BeOpen.com, a startup that failed in the dot-com bust, and Digital Creations, Python 2.0 was released in October 2000. In 2001, the Python Software Foundation was created to oversee and coordinate the further development of the Python language, and the foundation maintains the language to the present day. In 2008, Python 3.0, a major, backward, incompatible version, was released. Given the prevalence of Python 2, however, version 2.7 is being maintained alongside 3.0 and, although the change to the "print" command alone ensures that practically all 2.x programs will not work with 3.x, the community has made extensive efforts to make things work. Features in 3.x can be ported into 2.x using the `from __future__ import name_of_function` so that you can take advantage of the new features without having to completely refactor your code. In the spirit of Python, developers are focusing on flexibility and extensibility rather than on world domination.

Moving from Van Rossum hacking it together in his basement to make his other job easier, Python is now maintained as an open-source project by a bevy of developers (these people and any especially skilled Python coders are affectionately called Pythonistas; code written in the general style of the Python community, meanwhile, is called Pythonic) with a large number of specialized implementations. The language is now used for applications from film to web development to scientific computing and, specific to this work, libraries. All of this makes for a vibrant community with tools to fit a wide range of uses.

ENVIRONMENT AND SETUP

Setting up Python on a local machine will vary depending on the type of operating system being used. While Python can be installed and run on more than a dozen operating systems (https://www.python.org/download/other/), initial instructions on three of the more common operating systems—Linux, Macintosh, and Windows—are included below.

Linux

Some version of Python, typically Python 2.7, is already included with a number of the most popular Linux distributions, including Debian, Fedora, and Gentoo. However, not every installation will include a full set of features. If you want to use Python 3.0 or later, you will want to get it from your operating system's package repository; on Ubuntu, that might look like `sudo apt-get install python3`.

Macintosh

As of Mac OS X Yosemite, Python 2.7 is included out of the box. It's very straightforward to begin writing command line prompts from the Terminal, as Python commands can be entered from any directory. If you want a different version or Python is not installed, visit https://www.python.org/downloads/mac-osx/ and download the installer for the version of Python you want.

Windows

Unlike its UNIX-based counterparts, Windows does not ship with a version of Python installed. However, installation is typically quick and painless. Simply go to Python.org (https://www.python.org/downloads/), decide which version you would prefer (it is generally advised to take the most recent release in either the 2.7 or 3 lines, unless you have a specific reason not to), and run the .exe file. This will install Python, the collection of modules known as the Python Standard Library, and the basic Python text editor IDLE. While you will almost certainly want to enhance the environment you create your code in with better text editors or more modules, this simple install is all you need to get up and running writing Python code.

There are over seventy thousand freely available packages you can search through on PyPI (the Python Package Index) at pypi.python.org—these range from data parsing, to database manipulation, to packages that target specific end users. These packages are normally standardized in the way you'd go about installing them. As a general rule, a package installed for one version of Python may not be recognized by another version of Python. In short, if you are using Python 2.7, make sure to download packages for that version and not version 3.x, and if you are running more than one version of Python, the same package may not work for two versions. In most cases, tools like pip (described below) will take care of this for you, but it's an important aspect to keep in mind.

Packages in Python can be downloaded and used in a variety of ways, but by far the easiest and most common is to use a Python utility called pip. Pip is a package manager included with Python 2.7.9 and 3.4 onward, and, for earlier versions, it is easily downloaded and installed (https://pip.pypa.io/en/latest/installing.html). After following the instructions to install it, adding new modules is often as easy as opening your command line and issuing the command `pip install my_package`. You can use PyPI to find packages (this is the resource pip pulls from), but you will also often hear about packages on StackOverflow or other places where Python is discussed. To use a package, put `import my_package` at the top of your Python file, and you will have access to all the functionality provided. We will see several examples of this below as importing packages is one of the most common tasks in Python.

To truly see the power of packages, let's take an example from the documentation for Requests (Reitz 2011), one of the most popular Python packages. Requests allows us to make HTTP requests, abstracting away most of the details so we can just do what we came here for. Using Python's built-in urllib2 functionality, making a web request to GitHub might look like this:

```
import urllib2
gh_url = 'https://api.github.com'
req = urllib2.Request(gh_url)
password_manager = urllib2.HTTPPasswordMgrWithDefaultRealm()
password_manager.add_password(None, gh_url, 'user', 'pass')

auth_manager = urllib2.HTTPBasicAuthHandler(password_
manager)
opener = urllib2.build_opener(auth_manager)
```

```
urllib2.install_opener(opener)
handler = urllib2.urlopen(req)
print handler.getcode()
print handler.headers.getheader('content-type')
```

Don't worry if this code doesn't mean anything to you, as its purpose in life is to display the convoluted code you would have to write using just the standard tools to make a simple HTTP request to GitHub, then check the status code returned and the type of content returned. It's supposed to make you scratch your head, especially if you're just getting started. To make our lives better, let's install Requests. Open your command prompt and type `pip install requests`. Now the code we can write is:

```
import requests
r = requests.get('https://api.github.com', auth=('user', 'pass'))
print r.status_code
print r.headers['content-type']
```

If you've never seen Python code before, you might still guess what this code does. It imports something called requests, then uses that to get information from api.github.com, using a username and password (here called dummy variables "user" and "pass"). Then it prints the status code and part of the headers. Thanks to Kenneth Reitz making and freely releasing this library, we can write code that is understandable and much easier to use in a fraction of the time.

Python 2 versus Python 3

In late 2008, Python 3 was released. This new version was backward incompatible with past versions of Python, which ended with version 2.7. A number of improvements to the language were included with the Python 3.0 release, including better Unicode support, cleaning up past deprecations, and building in tools to assist developers new to the language in learning it better.

At the time of its release, Python 3 was declared the future of the language; however, because it was not backward compatible with previous versions of the language, many people who had been reliant on version 2.7 found that they needed to upgrade their applications. Others embraced the future of the language and used the newer Python 3 in all new developments. It is, however, possible to have multiple versions running on the same machine. Since Python 2.7 comes installed natively on a number of machines (see previous section), it may be necessary to install Python 3 separately. These two versions can run independently, but packages will need to be installed separately as well—one package won't work for both platforms. This is true for pip as well. However, with a little configuration, you can easily just keep track by using commands like `pip2` or `python3` when you want to run a specific version.

USES

Python's flexibility makes it appropriate for a variety of uses. Popular services such as Google, YouTube, and Dropbox code large-scale projects with it for both web and desktop environments. Closer to home in libraries, the Evergreen open-source ILS, though written largely with Perl, uses Python for some development tasks. However, Python's low barrier to entry makes it a particularly good fit for smaller projects to automate common tasks, such as web scraping, text analysis, or working with MARC records, and robust web frameworks, such as Django, make it a good option for CMSs and web development.

Before even getting outside the standard library, Python serves as a wonderful tool for quick data analysis. If you have serial holdings records from a vendor that aren't matching what you have in your ILS, and you do not want to manually cross-check hundreds of records, you can download a CSV file of the holdings from both systems and use Python to compare them to see where the discrepancies are. In a world of distributed systems and holdings coming from a wide variety of sources, the ability to do this kind of quick, custom, automated analysis can give you back hours of your workday.

In addition to its large standard library (set of available scripts), there are a number of third-party libraries that can make complex tasks simple and routine tasks almost effortless. For example, web-scraping libraries, such as Scrapy, can make website audits much more streamlined. Rather than going through each page and recording what the page is about, who authored the page, when it was last updated, and so on, you can use Scrapy to make a Python program that knows what kind of information is being looked for, where on pages to find that information, and what pages in a domain it should and shouldn't follow. Combined with built-in duplicate removal and output to several common formats, you can have an XML listing of pertinent information with less than an hour of work and thirty lines of coding.

With the XML file in hand, you may feel daunted by the sheer size, not having realized that your library's site was well over a thousand pages of content once you count all those LibGuides. Another Python library, NLTK (Natural Language ToolKit), can help with the analysis. Using NLTK, you can run an analysis over the entire audit. Thus, if your institution used to be a college but recently became a university, you can see how often and where "college" is referenced. If you are looking to institute a style guide, you can run an analysis that will tell you the fifty most common words used on your site and the context for some of them so you know how the current language fits. As with Scrapy, using the NLTK library makes it easy to get this kind of information without writing much code; ten lines and you know exactly which pages discuss lumberjacks and where you encounter Spam (sorry, couldn't help myself).

One of the most beneficial applications of Python in libraries, specific for catalogers or technical services workflows, is in the use of PyMARC—a Python library written to access, create, and manipulate raw binary MARC data. This library of PyMARC functions allows one to read in a .mrc file of MARC records, extract fields or subfields out of the records, modify fields and subfields by changing or removing them, and add new fields to the records. Based on specified criteria and field data, you can analyze the MARC data and write out reports to text files, which can be used for statistics or error analysis for batch clean-up projects. This ability to programmatically work with data can save a large amount of time, and, while tools such as MarcEdit can do large amounts of batch processing, learning PyMARC both gives greater freedom and, as mentioned, allows calling from batch scripts, such that it can be one of a number of things you automate together.

PROS AND CONS

As noted, there are many advantages to selecting Python as one's programming language of choice. Python generally comes preinstalled on most current operating systems, excluding Windows, so there is not a lot of setup in order to run your first script. For absolute beginners working on the command line, it may seem daunting at first to not be working in a GUI (graphical user interface) environment, but this is true for any language, and those fears are quickly overcome with just a little bit of exposure to the commands needed for basic operations.

While Python can be used to perform very complex workflows or build elaborate frameworks, it also allows beginners to write short, simple scripts that can create powerful results. Repetitive and mundane tasks that would normally take hours to perform manually can be completed in seconds. Additionally, the Python community is highly robust, creating packages and offering help so that any questions you might have will quite possibly already be answered, with code examples, a note about syntax, and a joke or two.

One aspect of Python that can be both a help and a hindrance is its use of significant white space. In other words, the way you indent your code changes how it is run (http://www.secnetix.de/olli/Python/block_indentation .hawk). Rather than using curly brackets or other syntax to express nested code blocks, Python uses tabs or spaces at the beginnings of lines to distinguish when a block of code starts or stops. For example, a set of *if/else* statements might look something like this:

```
if x == 1:
        print "x is odd"
elif x == 2:
        print "x is even"
else:
        print "I don't know what x is"
```

This is different from many other programming languages, but Python places a high value on readability and making things easier for humans. Thus, while it will take some getting used to and may have you yelling at your screen, in the long run this feature of the language makes your code more readable and easier to work with.

Another confusion beginners sometimes encounter is the difference between running Python commands directly in the Python shell (i.e., when the prompt begins with >>>) versus calling and running a full Python script using the python command and the script file name from the prompt (here a Windows DOS prompt): C:\> python myPythonScript.py. The Python shell allows you to check how a function operates before using it, or work out some nasty bit of code in an interactive environment. It's a useful feature, but none of your brilliant code will be saved, so once you've used the prompt to work something out, be sure to move it to a .py file and save it to be used in the future as shown above.

EXAMPLES

Python for Comparing Holdings

An area where Python excels is the writing of relatively short scripts to automate routine tasks. For instance, if we have a list of holdings from a vendor and we want to check these against holdings in our catalog, the task becomes onerous with even a modest number of holdings. However, with Python we can quickly write a script to automate our task, freeing us up to get another cup of coffee.

```
from_vendor = ['1234-5678', '2345-6789', '3456-7890']
from_catalog = ['1234-5678', '2345-6789', '3456-7890',
'1111-2222']
```

```
for issn in from_catalog:
        if issn not in from_vendor:
                print issn
```

This example demonstrates one very simple way to go about this. We make two variables called `from_vendor` and `from_catalog` and put a list of ISSN numbers in those variables (in Python, square brackets usually mean a list, which is quite literally just a list of data points separated by commas; also, these data points can be anything, so `['a', 'number', 3]` is a perfectly valid list). After that we compare the two lists using a `for` loop. The way Python is written is sometimes called "executable pseudocode" because the language's syntax tends much more toward plain English than most programming languages, and this code might give you some idea why.

Once we have our two lists of ISSN numbers, we simply say, "for every ISSN in the list called `from_catalog`, check to see if it is not in the list called `from_vendor` and print those to the screen." While this example shows us that Python can quickly do comparisons, it doesn't provide much utility over just doing the comparison ourselves, especially if we have to manually type in both sets of ISSNs by hand, which could get tiresome and time consuming with a whole library's worth of ISSNs. Luckily, Python makes it quick and easy to level up this simple script to handle larger sets of data, say by comparing the contents of two CSV files containing thousands of ISSN numbers each. For the sake of simplicity, we will assume that we have two CSV files, one from our catalog and one from a vendor, and that each has a single piece of information, the ISSN of a journal, in each row, as delimited by a comma. To get these out of the CSV file and into Python, we might do the following:

```
import csv

with open('issns_from_catalog.csv_from_catalog.csv', 'r')
as f:
        catalog_reader = csv.reader(f, delimiter=',')
        from_catalog = list(catalog_reader)

with open('issns_from_vendor.csv_from_vendor.csv', 'r') as
f:
        vendor_reader = csv.reader(f, delimiter=',')
        from_vendor = list(vendor_reader)
```

To work with CSV data, we first `import` the `csv` package, which is just a set of prewritten functions and is part of Python's base installation. Then we use the same code twice to open the files `issns_from_catalog.csv` and `issns_from_vendor.csv`, respectively, opening each using the `'r'` parameter to specify for reading only and calling each `f` (we can call them anything we want at this point; `f` is just a common convention for a variable name when opening a file). We then use the `csv` package we imported above to use a function called `reader`, which is predefined code that knows how to get information out of the CSV files we just opened, and we store the CSV data in variables called `catalog_reader` and `vendor_reader`. Finally, we create our `from_catalog` and `from_vendor` variables, which will work essentially the same as those same variables we wrote by hand earlier. To do this, we use the `list` function, which tells Python to take the CSV file we read with `csv.reader` and make it a Python list like the ones we typed out earlier. As a side note, any time you see yourself repeating code like we did above, you should be thinking about making it into a *function* to reuse your code, which you can read all about in the suggested resources below.

Next, we can reuse our comparison code from above with a slight modification. Rather than printing all of the nonmatching ISSNs to the screen, we will collect them in their own list.

```
not_in_both = []
for issn in from_catalog:
        if issn not in from_vendor:
                not_in_both.append(issn)
```

As you can see, this code works very similarly to the code above. Only now we are making an empty list called `not_in_both` first by using empty brackets (in Python, and many other languages, you can give yourself an empty version of a container by using empty brackets or empty curly braces; these are useful when you want a list but you want to fill it up as you go along rather than all at once), and we will fill this list up as we go with ISSNs that are in `from_catalog` but not in `from_vendor`. Once we do our check, we place the ISSNs into `not_in_both` using `.append`, which just appends an item onto the end of a list.

For a more physical example of `.append`, imagine we have a list called `numbers` with 1, 2, and 3 in it, like `numbers = [1,2,3]`. If we wanted to add 4 to that list, using `numbers.append(4)` would give us the list `[1,2,3,4]`. So by the end of this segment of code, we have gone through thousands of journal ISSNs and made a list of the ones that our catalog claims we have access to but our vendor does not have listed. Not bad for roughly eleven lines of code.

One final improvement we might want to make is to create a new file that will list all of these ISSNs so we can send them to our cataloger or vendor to get to the bottom of the discrepancy. To do this, we will open one more file similarly to how we opened the CSV files before, with a key difference.

```
with open('compared_lists.txt', 'w') as f:
    for issn in not_in_both:
        f.write(issn+'\n')
```

We start very similarly to opening the CSV files above, using `with open` and a file name to actually open a file, only this time we use the parameter `'w'` to tell Python we want to *write* to this file rather than `'r'` to *read* from it (please note: any time you open a file with `'w'`, anything currently in that file will be deleted before anything new is added, so be careful not to over-write important information). We then use `for` to go over everything in the `not_in_both` list we just made. For each item in that list, we tell Python to write the ISSN to the file we are calling `f` and add a newline (`/n`) so each ISSN is on its own line. As an added bonus, you don't even have to worry about a file named `compared_lists.txt` existing before you open it; if it does not already exist, Python will just create it for you.

We can pull all of our pieces together to have a small program that can automate a task that could take human eyes hours. If everything does not make complete sense yet, stick with it and know that the particulars of lists, working with files, packages, functions, and so on will become clear as you learn and practice. Even if it isn't clear yet, we hope you can see that Python is an excellent language for writing these short utility programs that can automate common tasks, and that with only about fourteen lines of code, we have opened two files, gotten thousands of pieces of information out of them, compared them, and made a new file that lists our results.

Here is the full program we just created:

```
import csv
with open('issns_from_catalog.cvs', 'r') as f:
    catalog_reader = csv.reader(f, delimiter=',')
    from_catalog = list(catalog_reader)

with open('issns_from_vendor.csv', 'r') as f:
    vendor_reader = csv.reader(f, delimiter=',')
    from_vendor = list(vendor_reader)
not_in_both = []
for issn in from_catalog:
    if issn not in from_vendor:
        not_in_both.append(issn)
with open('compared_lists.txt', 'w') as f:
    for issn in not_in_both:
        f.write(issn+'\n')
```

PyMARC for Batch Processing MARC Records

For cataloging librarians, the PyMARC module is especially useful for batch processing sets of MARC records and automating technical services workflows. PyMARC can be downloaded by running the command `pip install pymarc`. You can find documentation on the PyMARC GitHub page at https://github.com/edsu/pymarc. PyMARC includes a number of core functions that allow you to extract, analyze, add, or remove fields and subfields in raw binary MARC record data. These core functions are somewhat divided by level of operation, such as file level, record level, or field level.

For example, there are file-level functions that allow you to read in or write out a file of binary MARC records in .mrc format—the `MARCReader()` and `MARCWriter()` functions. Both of these functions require the name of a .mrc file as the parameter passed to the function, as follows:

```
marc_recs_in = pymarc.MARCReader(file('marc_input.mrc'))
marc_recs_out = pymarc.MARCWriter(file('marc_output.mrc',
'w'))
```

Note that the file parameter for the `MARCWriter()` function also needs the attribute `'w'` so that the specified file name is writable when it is created—meaning that MARC records can be "written into" the .mrc file. There are additional, optional parameters that can be used with the `MARCReader()` function when reading in a file of MARC records which help to handle Unicode and MARC8 versus UTF8 issues, setting the parameters `to_unicode` and `force_utf8` equal to true:

```
marc_recs_in = pymarc.MARCReader(file('marc_input.mrc'),
to_unicode=True, force_utf8=True)
```

At the record level, the most common functions involve one of three tasks:

1. Getting fields out of a record using `record.get_fields([MARC_tag])`
2. Removing a field from a record using `record.remove_field([field_object])`
3. Adding a field to a record using `record.add_ordered_field([field_object])`

The `get_fields()` function accepts one or more MARC field tag numbers separated by commas and returns each instance of those fields in a list variable as PyMARC "field object" types. The `remove_field()` function takes a PyMARC field object as an argument and removes the matching object. And the `add_ordered_field()` function takes a field object that you would build up in your program and adds it to your MARC record.

Field-level functions work in much the same way as record-level functions, except you are getting, setting, or deleting subfields from a field rather than fields from a record. The common field-level functions are:

1. Getting subfields out of a field using `field.get_subfields([subfield_code])`
2. Removing a subfield from a field using `field.delete_subfield([subfield_code])`
3. Adding a subfield to a field using `field.add_subfield([subfield_code], [subfield_content])`

So consider that you wanted to add a placeholder record for this book until you get the chance to do some full-level cataloging on it. You would start by importing any module you might need, in this case `pymarc`, then creating a new record for our book. It will start as a blank "record object" to which we will add fields.

```
import pymarc
new_record = pymarc.Record()
```

First, there is nothing special about naming it `new_record`. It could have been called `Gryffindor` and the program would run just as well, but it is generally good practice to name things in a way that describes what they are. Note that, since the `Record()` function comes from the `pymarc` module, we have to tell Python to get `Record()` out of there by prefacing it with `pymarc`.

Next, we will create a new field to populate our record using the `Field()` function:

```
new_field_245 = pymarc.Field(
     tag = '245',
     indicators = ['0','0'],
     subfields = ['a', 'Programming for librarians /',
          'c', 'edited by Beth Thomsett-Scott.']
)
```

Here we just tell Python this is going to be a field. Then we give it some information about the field including the MARC tag number, indicator values, and a list of the subfields and their content. As in most programming languages, text strings are very literal, so notice that the punctuation must be included in the subfield content value in order to create the subfields according to standardized AACR rules (http://www.aacr2.org/). The above `Field()` command creates the following 245 title field and assigns it to our variable called `new_field_245`:

```
245 0 0 $aProgramming for librarians / $cedited by Beth
Thomsett-Scott.
```

We can do this for any number of fields. For instance, since we know the editor, we can create a 700 personal name field for her:

```
new_field_700 = pymarc.Field(
tag = '700',
indicators = ['1',' '],
subfields = ['a', 'Thomsett-Scott, Beth C.']
)
```

Finally, we want to add both of these fields to our record, and write that record to a file (as in the first example given in this chapter).

```
new_record.add_ordered_field(new_field_245)
new_record.add_ordered_field(new_field_700)
with open('output.mrc', 'w') as f:
     f.write(new_record.as_marc())
```

This tells Python to add both of the fields we created to our record in field number order using the `add_ordered_field()` function, make sure it is in the correct format by running `as_marc()`, then write that record to a file called `output.mrc`. With that, we just programmatically created a MARC record in a script that can be quickly leveled up to run through and create hundreds at a time by pulling the field data (i.e., titles and authors) from a CSV file or other data source. The full script for creating this new brief record is put together below.

```
import pymarc
new_record = pymarc.Record()

new_field_245 = pymarc.Field(
     tag = '245',
     indicators = ['0','0'],
     subfields = ['a', 'Programming for librarians /',
     'c', 'edited by Beth Thomsett-Scott.']
)
new_field_700 = pymarc.Field(
```

```
    tag = '700',
    indicators = ['1',' '],
    subfields = ['a', 'Thomsett-Scott, Beth C.']
)
new_record.add_ordered_field(new_field_245)
new_record.add_ordered_field(new_field_700)

with open('output.mrc', 'w') as f:
    f.write(new_record.as_marc())
```

SUMMARY

Python is an open-source, simple, flexible programming language that is used in everything from systems to web development. The language and the vibrant, active community that uses it place great value on code being readable and as obvious as possible; clarity is prized over cleverness and openness over concealment. This has led to the community releasing large amounts of open-source code, including library-specific packages like PyMARC, that make it easy to quickly accomplish tasks rather than reinventing the wheel. These same elements of clarity—it strongly encourages you to write well-written, readable code from the beginning—and depth make it a great first programming language to learn as well as a powerful and extensible language to use in large, complex projects.

BIBLIOGRAPHY

Lutz, Mark. 2013. *Learning Python.* 5th ed. Sebastopol, CA: O'Reilly Media.
Peters, Tim. 2004. "The Zen of Python." August 19. https://www.python.org/dev/peps/pep-0020/.
Reitz, Kenneth. 2011. "0_urllib2.py." GitHub Gist. https://gist.github.com/kennethreitz/973705.
Van Rossum, Guido. 2009–2013. *The History of Python.* http://python-history.blogspot.com/.

RECOMMENDED RESOURCES

Code Academy. https://www.codecademy.com/. The favorite first stop of many a self-taught programmer, Code Academy's Python course will introduce you to the major points of the language. Additionally, you can look at some of its API courses to see how Python can interact with the web.

Hitchhiker's Guide to Python. http://docs.python-guide.org/en/latest/. A self-proclaimed *opinionated* way to learn Python, this guide focuses not only on learning the language, but how to write *Pythonic* code. Making use of the official Python style guide, this is a great resource for writing clean, reusable code like a *Pythonista.*

Learning Python the Hard Way. http://learnpythonthehardway.org/. Available for purchase or free online, this presents a practical way to learn Python, moving at a deliberate pace to solidify concepts. An excellent way to get used to both syntax and programming principles.

Library Juice (courses on Python). The library professional development service periodically offers courses to get you started using Python for various library tasks.

Two Scoops of Django. A standard reference if you want to get up and running doing web development in Python. This book will show you how to build web applications and, importantly, how to do it well.

Chapter Three

Ruby

Ashley Blewer and Jessica Rudder

HISTORY AND DEVELOPMENT

What is Ruby and how is it different from other languages? In the official documentation, Ruby is described as the following: "A dynamic, open source programming language with a focus on simplicity and productivity. It has an elegant syntax that is natural to read and easy to write" (https://www .ruby-lang.org/en/). Now let's break that description down so we can really understand its meaning.

Ruby is a *dynamic* language—also referred to as a scripting language. This means that programs written in Ruby are interpreted (read) line-by-line as they are being executed. This is in contrast to compiled languages where the source code is transformed from one programming language (the source language) into another computer language (the target language) before the program can be run. Scripting languages, such as Ruby, tend to be easier for learners to pick up; however, the tradeoff is that they generally run slower than compiled languages.

Ruby is also an *open-source* language. When a program is open source, the source code is available to the public for free. You can use it as is or modify the code as needed. If you make a change that you find useful, you can upload your changes for other people to use. The entire source code for the language is available online. Seriously! You can go view it here: https:// github.com/ruby/ruby.

Thirdly, Ruby is an *object-oriented* language. Object-oriented programming languages are based on the concept of "objects," which are data structures, and "methods," which are procedures used to change or utilize those objects. By definition, languages built in this way use "objects." To use a spoken language analogy, these objects can be thought of as nouns. And the "methods" could be considered verbs.

Now that we have defined Ruby, let us take a quick look at its history. By the early 1990s, there were a wide variety of programming languages in existence from C (a low-level language widely used for system programming) to Python (a language that functions similarly to Ruby). Unlike many other languages that were developed solely to fit a specific programming need, Ruby was created with both a functional and an aesthetic purpose in mind.

Ruby was designed by Yukihiro Matsumoto (colloquially known as Matz) in the mid-1990s. Although he was familiar with Perl, Matz did not believe it would be able to create reliable, maintainable programs in a production environment. He also knew Python but didn't feel that it was a true object-oriented language, which was a very important characteristic for him. According to Matsumoto, "As a language maniac and [object-oriented] fan for 15 years, I really wanted a genuine object-oriented, easy-to-use scripting language. I looked for but couldn't find one. So I decided to make it" (Matsumoto 1999).

Matsumoto also wanted to create a beautiful language that would be a joy to program in. He felt that most computer languages place a burden on the human writing the code in order to remove a burden from the computer. This resulted in programming being unnecessarily hard. Matz believed that the focus needed to be on people rather than machines, so his goal was to create a language that would make programming enjoyable whether you were a beginner or had been programming for years. To this end, he designed Ruby according to the following three principles:

Principle of Conciseness: Matsumoto felt that computers should be able to do a lot of work with very few orders. By requiring the computer to do more heavy lifting (like figuring out variable types and handling memory management) with fewer commands written by the programmer, it reduced both the memory and time burden of writing code. To see this in action, you can compare a "Hello, World" code from Java, a popular object-oriented language, and Ruby. In Java, the code looks like this:

```
class HelloWorld {
     public static void main(String[] args) {
          System.out.println("Hello World!");
}
}
```

In Ruby:

```
puts "Hello, World!"
```

Both sets of code produce the same result. The text `Hello, World!` will be printed to the screen. The Ruby code is much shorter and easier for a programmer to both write and understand.

Principle of Consistency: Ruby is said to follow the principle of least astonishment (POLA), meaning it should behave in such a way as to minimize confusion for people writing in it. Ruby is intended to be as simple as possible, while remaining deep, in order to maximize ease of use. Ruby isn't meant just to be simple—Ruby is meant to be *natural* to read, in the same way that noncomputer languages should be natural.

```
5.times do
     puts "Hello, World!"
end
```

Even someone without programming experience can read the code above and have a good sense of what that code would do if it were run.

Principle of Flexibility: Matsumoto believed that languages (including computer languages) were meant to express thoughts. Instead of restricting human thought, the language should facilitate it. As such, Ruby was created with a small, unchangeable core syntax and the ability to extend the language as needed and desired throughout libraries. In contrast to Python, which emphasizes there being "one right way" of completing a task, Ruby tries to provide many approaches so that the developer can find one that fits him or her best. One great example is the code for doing a task multiple times:

```
1. 10.times do
     puts "Ruby is flexible!"
end

2. (1..10).each { puts "Ruby is flexible!"}

3. for i in 1..10 do
     puts "Ruby is flexible!"
end

4. 1.upto(10) { puts "Ruby is flexible!"}
```

The result of the four examples above is the same. In each case, the phrase `Ruby is flexible!` appears ten times. This flexibility can be especially useful to people who are new to Ruby as it allows them to approach the same problem from multiple angles.

Beyond the theory behind the language's development, Ruby was influenced by Perl, Smalltalk, Eiffel, Ada, and Lisp, other object-oriented programming languages. The syntax is similar to Perl, and the semantics are similar to Smalltalk.

ENVIRONMENT AND SETUP

Ruby comes packaged by default on Mac machines. Additional versions of Ruby and other relevant programs can be installed using HomeBrew (http://brew.sh/), a package manager for Mac operating systems. This package manager is built in Ruby! If you are using a Windows machine, you will have to install Ruby because it is not natively packaged. There is a project called RubyInstaller that can help (http://rubyinstaller.org/) facilitate this installation.

To start using Ruby immediately, you can open up the Interactive Ruby Shell, or IRB. IRB comes packaged with Ruby, so it is installed when Ruby is installed. The ability to get started quickly and to start writing code immediately after the installation of the language is one of Ruby's strengths.

The IRB is a "shell" that allows you to safely write and test Ruby code in your computer's Terminal. On Macs, typing `irb` will open it up on your screen. Typing `quit` will quit the program and take you back to your regular Terminal screen. Ctrl-D will also quit the program. To open up the IRB on a Windows machine, you can click Start and select Interactive Ruby from your menu.

You can try out programming in Ruby by opening up IRB and entering the following code:

```
name = "Ruby programmer"
puts "Hello, #{name}!"
```

In this mini program, `name` is a "variable," a type of storage location, which now contains the phrase "Ruby programmer." The second line tells Ruby to insert the contents of the variable `name` into the phrase "Hello, ____!" and output the final phrase `"Hello, Ruby programmer!"` to the screen.

When you exit the IRB, your code will disappear as well. Instead of using the IRB, you can also write a Ruby program. Writing Ruby in a text editor, such as SublimeText, Atom, or TextWrangler, and saving it as an .rb file will create a Ruby script file. This file can then be run on the command line by typing `ruby filename.rb` and hitting enter. Try this out using the code from the IRB section above. You should see `"Hello, Ruby programmer!"` in your terminal after you run your file. Note that Microsoft Word will not work as a text editor in this situation due to the extra information it puts into files, which will cause the program not to run.

Ruby is a wonderful language that allows you to write programs quickly and efficiently. Another excellent feature of Ruby is the concept of gems. Gems are bundled libraries of Ruby code that are easy to install and use in projects. Even a large web framework, such as Ruby on Rails, is packaged as a Ruby gem and can be downloaded and installed with only one line of code: `gem install rails`. Anyone can create a gem and share it with the world through RubyGems.org, a gem hosting service for the Ruby community.

USES

Ruby is most commonly used in web development, and the Ruby on Rails framework is based on the Ruby programming language. Smaller frameworks, including Sinatra and Middleman, allow dynamic websites to be created easily and are powered by Ruby. Ruby is very effective at powering the server side of websites, which allows your computer to connect to a server that can deliver the data you need.

Because Ruby is natively built into Macs and easy to install on Windows machines, it is useful for parsing small data sets. For example, if you have a thousand records containing patron data but you only need to access their email addresses, you can write a small script that will take that data and export only the email addresses to a new file for use in a newsletter.

Several large frameworks used in library and information sciences are based on Ruby. Project Blacklight, Hydra, and Avalon are all built with Ruby; thus having even a basic knowledge of how Ruby works will help with the installation, development, and maintenance of these frameworks.

Project Blacklight (http://projectblacklight.org/) is an open-source project that allows for access and discovery of library materials. It runs on Ruby on Rails and works with Apache Solr to make searching library collections easier. Blacklight is bundled as a gem that can then be used when creating a new Rails instance.

Project Hydra (http://projecthydra.org/) is a digital repository with software components built as Ruby gems. Hydra is used as a digital asset management framework as well as a framework for providing access to digital collections. Like Blacklight, Hydra is bundled as a gem that works with Rails and several other gems to create the digital repository.

Avalon Media System (http://www.avalonmediasystem.org/) is based on Project Hydra and is intended to handle a library or archive's digital audio and visual assets, and provide access to those assets via a web interface. The project was created and is led by Indiana University Bloomington and North-western University after being funded in part by a two-year grant from the Andrew W. Mellon Foundation.

Smaller scripts and gems have been created to optimize library-focused work. Examples are ruby-oai, a Ruby library for building OAI-PMH clients and servers (https://github.com/code4lib/ruby-oai); nypl-collections, a gem for easily accessing the digital collections held at the New York Public Library (https://rubygems.org/gems/nypl-collections); and, marc, a gem for (you guessed it) working with MARC catalog records (https://rubygems.org/gems/marc/versions/1.0.0).

PROS AND CONS

The language of Ruby strives to be human readable, which is perhaps its greatest strength. The goal of Ruby is not just to be simple, but to be natural in the same way that reading English is natural to native English speakers. Ruby is simple to understand but complex when understanding its full potential.

```
5. times do
      puts "I love Ruby!"
end
```

With a simple script such as this, you can guess what is going to to happen even if you have no prior experience programming. This code will print I love Ruby! to the screen five times.

Installation is easy, both the language and any language libraries that you may want to install. Ruby is packaged natively on Macs, and there are installation instructions for Windows- or Linux-based machines. Libraries of code, known as gems, are easy to install using the gem install command on the command line. Given the above comments, Ruby is a very suitable language for beginners since a beginner can learn the core concepts of programming without being bogged down with difficult syntax or environment setup errors.

Beyond the code itself, Ruby has a strong and dedicated community of users and developers. Since Ruby is open source, anyone can improve the language or create libraries that make it easier for other people to use the language.

Ruby is a great choice for beginners but may not be the best choice in the long term, depending on the reason for learning a programming language. For instance, Ruby is great for developing code meant for the web, but JavaScript is a powerful language built for and on the web. JavaScript may, therefore, be a more effective long-term choice if your main reason for learning to code is to make websites.

When it comes to scaling web applications to become Facebook sized, Ruby is "slower" than what is necessary, depending on the type of data deployed and if it needs to be live while updating. However, Codecademy, AirBNB, and other major sites run on Ruby on Rails. Every operation in Ruby—even integer addition—is done by invoking methods, so the cost to search and invoke methods cannot be ignored, especially for simple programs. When programs get bigger and more complex, however, no significant performance difference should arise as a result of methods (Matsumoto 2000).

JavaScript has had better libraries built around data visualization. Ruby still lacks the ability to write code that creates complex visualizations. This isn't because there is anything wrong with the Ruby language itself, but unfortunately the needed libraries have not been built by Ruby programmers.

Ruby and Python are very similar programming languages. Python might be a better fit over Ruby if the primary focus is on science-based learning. Python is used more frequently for research and data science, and the community around Python has supported these needs.

EXAMPLES

Parsing JSON Data

JSON stands for JavaScript Object Notation. It was built to serve as a lightweight way to transfer data from one system to another. The design is intended to be easy for humans to read and write and easy for computers to parse and create. It is text based and language agnostic, meaning that your JSON can be used in programs written in Ruby, Python, C++, and other languages.

Here is some sample JSON taken from Twitter's API documentation (https://dev.twitter.com/rest/reference/get/statuses/show/:id):

```
{
"coordinates": null,
"favorited": false,
"truncated": false,
"created_at": "Wed Jun 06 20:07:10 +0000 2012",
"id_str": "210462857140252672",
"entities": {
"urls": [
{
"expanded_url": "https://dev.twitter.com/terms/display-guidelines",
"url": "https://t.co/Ed4omjYs",
```

```
"indices": [
76,
97
],
"display_url": "dev.twitter.com/terms/display-\u2026"
}
],
"hashtags": [
}
"text": "Twitterbird",
"indices": [
19,
31
]
}
],
"user_mentions": [

]
},
"in_reply_to_user_id_str": null,
"contributors": [
14927800
],
"text": "Along with our new #Twitterbird, we've also
updated our Display Guidelines: https://t.co/Ed4omjYs ^JC",
"retweet_count": 66,
"in_reply_to_status_id_str": null,
"id": 210462857140252672,
"geo": null,
"retweeted": true,
"possibly_sensitive": false,
"in_reply_to_user_id": null,
"place": null,
"user": {
"profile_sidebar_fill_color": "DDEEF6",
"profile_sidebar_border_color": "C0DEED",
"profile_background_tile": false,
"name": "Twitter API",
"profile_image_url":"http://a0.twimg.com/profile_images/2284
174872/7df3h38zabcvjylnyfe3_normal.png",
"created_at": "Wed May 23 06:01:13 +0000 2007",
"location": "San Francisco, CA",
"follow_request_sent": false,
"profile_link_color": "0084B4",
"is_translator": false,
"id_str": "6253282",
```

```
"entities": {
"url": {
"urls": [
{
"expanded_url": null,
"url": "http://dev.twitter.com",
"indices": [
0,
22
]
}
]
},
"description": {
"urls": [
]
}
},
"default_profile": true,
"contributors_enabled": true,
"favourites_count": 24,
"url": "http://dev.twitter.com",
"profile_image_url_https":"https://si0.twimg.com/profile_ima
ges/2284174872/7df3h38zabcvjylnyfe3_normal.png",
"utc_offset": -28800,
"id": 6253282,
"profile_use_background_image": true,
"listed_count": 10774,
"profile_text_color": "333333",
"lang": "en",
"followers_count": 1212963,
"protected": false,
"notifications": null,
"profile_background_image_url_https":"https://si0.twimg.com/
images/themes/theme1/bg.png",
"profile_background_color": "C0DEED",
"verified": true,
"geo_enabled": true,
"time_zone": "Pacific Time (US & Canada)",
"description": "The Real Twitter API. I tweet about API
changes, service issues and happily answer questions about
Twitter and our API. Don't get an answer? It's on my
website.",
"default_profile_image": false,
"profile_background_image_url":"http://a0.twimg.com/images/
themes/theme1/bg.png",
"statuses_count": 3333,
```

```
"friends_count": 31,
"following": true,
"show_all_inline_media": false,
"screen_name": "twitterapi"
},
"in_reply_to_screen_name": null,
"source": "web",
"in_reply_to_status_id": null
}
```

Remember that the above is all of the metadata associated with just one tweet. Imagine that instead of having one JSON block like the above, you have thousands, all with different data values inside. It would be simpler if you could get all the information you need and not have to dig through ten thousand lines of curly brackets, right? Well, Ruby can help you do that.

Before you can begin working with JSON, you will need to install one of the JSON libraries created for Ruby. If you haven't already, you will need to run gem install 'json'. Then, at the top of your text document, include require 'json'. Open a valid JSON file in Ruby:

```
file = open('test.json')
```

Now the JSON must be read and parsed:

```
json = file.read
data = JSON.parse(json)
```

The above relies on the JSON library to modify the data in the necessary way to make it readable by Ruby. Now that the data has been modified, it can be organized. Here are some simple things we can do:

```
data[0]
# This will return the first tweet in a series
data[2]["text"]
# This will return the content of the third tweet in a
series
```

But what if we want to see more than just one tweet at a time? We can loop through the entire text to pull out the desired information.

```
data.each do |tweet|
p tweet["text"]
end
```

This will return the text (the "tweet" part of the tweet) of every JSON object. Each tweet has so much associated metadata that even more interesting information can be gathered using this similar method, like the number of retweets, geographic data, hashtags used, or author descriptions.

Scraping the Web with Nokogiri

What is web scraping? Web scraping is programmatically pulling data from the Internet so you can use the data in your own applications. Nokogiri is a Ruby gem that makes it easy to scrape the web for data. It is also an easy way to consistently grab data from various sources and have it all in one place for analysis. Nokogiri (from the Japanese word 鋸, for "saw") is an HTML, XML, SAX, and Reader parser. Among Nokogiri's many features is the ability to search documents via XPath or CSS3 selectors (http://www .nokogiri.org/).

To use Nokogiri, we will also need to use Open-URI. Open-URI is a module in Ruby that allows us to programmatically make http requests. It will allow us to easily open and parse the content of an HTML page via the command line.

You can write a file that performs all of these actions at once, or you can step through them with the tutorial using the IRB—remember that you can access this via the Mac Terminal by typing IRB or selecting it from the Start menu on a Windows machine. At the top of your file, you will need to require both of these libraries in order for your program to know that it needs them. This is as simple as adding the following lines of code to the top of your text document:

```
require 'nokogiri'
require 'open-uri'
```

Select a website of interest. For this example, we'll use the "Visiting the Library" page from the Library of Congress (figure 3.1). One you have your page selected, use Open-URI to open up the site. We do that like this:

```
html = open(http://www.loc.gov/visit/)
```

A temporary object should be printed to the screen. To parse that data with Nokogiri, we can run this:

```
nokogiri = Nokogiri::HTML(html)
```

Figure 3.1. "Visiting the Library" (Library of Congress).

This will put the contents of that website to the screen. Do you see what we are doing here? We are declaring a variable and naming it nokogiri (although you can name it anything you want, just like the HTML variable above).

Inspecting the web page's HTML, we can see that Tours, Exhibitions, and other headers use the h2 tag. If you wanted to quickly pull in this list without accessing the website, you can use Nokogiri.

Now that we have the website loaded into the variable nokogiri, we can get the contents out of the site. The line `title = nokogiri.css('h2')`. `text` will pull in all of the h2 tags on the page. The text will look a little messy because of the extra spaces in the code. Ruby will clean up that data.

```
title = nokogiri.css('h2').collect do |titles|
        titles.text.strip!
end
```

Now we not only have the titles we want, but we also have a lot of nil titles. This is from messy data on the site that didn't have anything inside of it. All of these blank tags returned nil.

```
[nil, nil, nil, nil, nil, nil, nil, nil, nil, nil, nil,
nil, nil, nil, nil, nil, nil, nil, nil, nil, nil, nil,
"Visiting the Library", "Tours", "Maps & Floor Plans",
```

```
"Dining", "Shopping", "Volunteer Opportunities", "Contact
Visitor Services", nil, nil, nil, nil]
```

We can clean that up quickly with Ruby as well by running the `compact!` method.

```
title.compact!
```

Now we have an array with all of the options we want:

```
["Visiting the Library", "Tours", "Maps & Floor Plans",
"Dining", "Shopping", "Volunteer Opportunities", "Contact
Visitor Services"]
```

This is a very simple example, but there are many ways to use Nokogiri to scrape the web and then manipulate the data easily with Ruby. You can test this out on your own website just by replacing the above example and the CSS with your own website and the objects you want to scrape. The web scraper is useful for sites that have repetitive data structures on different pages, sort of like the Library of Congress Subject Heading Authorities page (http://authorities.loc.gov/). Even if you change the URL you set up in Open-URI, you can still use the same code previously written in order to access any page. You can even set up a script that could scrape as many pages as you wanted.

SUMMARY

Ruby is a dynamic, object-oriented, open-source programming language that strives for simplicity and productivity. Ruby was developed with the goal of making a programming language that is a joy to work in. The three principles Ruby follows are the principle of conciseness, the principle of consistency, and the principle of flexibility. Library-centric web applications built on Ruby include Project Blacklight and Project Hydra, along with many other easy-to-use libraries of code, known as Ruby gems. Its active, caring community; simple but elegant syntax; and ease of setup and use make it an excellent programming language for a beginner.

BIBLIOGRAPHY

Matsumoto, Yukihiro. 1999. "ruby-talk:00382." June 4. http://marc.info/?l=ruby-talk&m=96398337724637&w=2.

————. 2000. "The Ruby Programming Language." InformIT, June 12. http://www
.informit.com/articles/article.aspx?p=18225&seqNum=2.

RECOMMENDED RESOURCES

Online Sources

HacketyHack.com: http://www.hackety.com/
Learn.co: https://learn.co/
Learn Ruby with the Neo Ruby Koans: http://rubykoans.com
Try Ruby: http://tryruby.org/
Why's (Poignant) Guide to Ruby: http://mislav.uniqpath.com/poignant-guide/

Books

Black, David A. 2014. *The Well-Grounded Rubyist.* Greenwich, CT: Manning.
Cooper, Peter. 2011. *Beginning Ruby: From Novice to Professional.* New York:
    Apress.
Fernandez, Obie, and Kevin Faustino. 2014. *The Rails 4 Way.* Boston: Addison-
    Wesley Professional.
Metz, Sandy. 2012. *Practical Object-Oriented Design in Ruby: An Agile Primer.*
    Boston: Addison-Wesley Professional.
Olsen, Russ. 2011. *Eloquent Ruby.* Boston: Addison-Wesley Professional.
Shaughnessy, Pat. 2013. *Ruby under a Microscope: An Illustrated Guide to Ruby
    Internals.* San Francisco: No Starch Press.

Chapter Four

JavaScript

Jason Bengtson and Eric Phetteplace

HISTORY AND DEVELOPMENT

Understanding JavaScript's history is an important step in comprehending the nature of the language. It was developed as a scripting language for web browsers by the Netscape Communications Corporation in 1995. Infamously, the original developer was given only ten days to design and code the entire language, a language that faced the technical challenges of being embedded within HyperText Markup Language (HTML) (Wood et al. 2014). In order to understand this complexity, consider that HTML relies on angle brackets around its tags, such as `<body>`, so even the use of the common mathematical symbols for greater than and less than comparisons posed difficulties for the new language's design. Given its hasty development and the challenges faced, it is no surprise that JavaScript has its share of oddities and outright errors. Despite this, JavaScript succeeded and is actually one of the most used programming languages on the planet, lauded by some for its expressiveness and innovative features.

When Netscape developers set about designing a scripting language for the browser, they wanted it to be approachable, particularly for new programmers (Wood et al. 2014). The design goals for the language focused on simplicity, making it possible to accomplish tasks with small amounts of code, and not requiring compilation. Compilation is the process of passing computer code to a "compiler" program that produces a binary executable. JavaScript borrowed its ideas from existing languages, such as Scheme, HyperTalk, and Smalltalk, rather than the more complex compiled languages of the time, including C and Java. The name itself is often a source of confusion: JavaScript bears no formal relation to Java. Rather, the JavaScript name was a sort of marketing gimmick aimed to associate the new scripting language with the popular Java language (Wood et al. 2014). While the two do bear some surface similarities, they are in fact very different in terms of both their philosophy and their use cases. In fact, while JavaScript is the commonly known name, the language is standardized as ECMAScript after the Ecma International organization, which presides over the standard.

JavaScript's fate has been bound to that of web browsers, for better and worse. Since JavaScript became used on websites across the globe shortly after its release, it was difficult to correct the language's initial defects. While other programming languages can release new compiler or interpreter programs that remove troublesome features or drastically alter their syntax, JavaScript's web-based nature makes its evolution arduous. Over time, web browsers developed inconsistent, competing, and occasionally flawed implementations of the language. With browsing as the language's primary use, it is difficult to discern language flaws from poorly designed browser features. After an initial set of updates that ended with the third edition of ECMAScript published in 1999, the language stagnated. A fourth edition was started but never completed due to disagreement among the authoring committee (Wood et al. 2014). However, browsers also drove the popularity of JavaScript and some of its most innovative uses.

Microsoft's Internet Explorer introduced what would become the XML-HttpRequest feature in the late 1990s (Flanagan 2011, 491–94). This browser feature is the foundation of so-called AJAX (an acronym for Asynchronous JavaScript and XML, though non-XML data formats can be used) programming, a lightweight technique for pulling data into web pages without requiring a full-page refresh. AJAX eventually spawned an influx of innovative web applications written in JavaScript, such as Outlook Web App, Gmail, and Google Maps. These dynamic applications constantly refreshed their data and intelligently responded to user input, a far cry from the set of interconnected but static documents that characterized the early web of the 1990s.

As sophisticated web applications were popularized, and Internet companies turned profits, JavaScript became a tremendously important language. Its stasis risked holding back the development of the web. Major tech companies took notice and starting pushing the language forward. Employees of Apple, Ebay, Google, Intel, Microsoft, and Mozilla are represented on the TC39 committee in charge of the ECMAScript standard (ECMAScript Wiki n.d.). A fresh wave of investment in the web resulted in an improved fifth edition of ECMAScript in 2009 and a massive influx of browser features loosely grouped under the term *HTML5*. HTML5 saw the web move even further from a document-based hypertext system to perhaps the premier site for cross-platform application development. JavaScript gained access to storage and databases, geolocation information, advanced geometric drawing and graphics capabilities, audio and video, and user hardware such as microphones and video cameras, previously the sole domain of browser plug-ins, such as Adobe Flash. Today, JavaScript is a robust and thriving language. New features are being rapidly developed for web browsers and the language itself. The language is starting to grow roots outside of the web browser with exciting new uses that are discussed below.

USES

JavaScript is primarily known for a single thing: making websites interactive. While other frameworks have attempted this—notably Java applets and Adobe Flash—they do so via browser plug-ins that a user must install, while JavaScript is included in every web browser in common use. Apple's decision not to allow Adobe Flash on the iPhone's Mobile Safari browser gave a large edge to JavaScript. It is widely recognized that using JavaScript is the best way to write cross-platform interactive websites, and this is the language's principal distinction.

Creating a multitab search box is a good example of JavaScript's capabilities. Multitab search boxes are a common feature of library websites since many libraries offer a number of different search engines: a catalog of books and media, a discovery layer that includes journal articles, a federated search over several separate search engines, a periodicals search, LibGuides, special collections, archives. Each of these offers different facets and instructions to the user, while putting the search forms one after another on your website takes up an enormous amount of space. A tabbed search that shows only one search form at a time saves space but still offers users access to a variety of search engines via the other tabs. These interfaces are implemented in JavaScript, which displays the appropriate search form when a tab is clicked.

Another JavaScript use that improves the search experience is filtering and sorting search results in the web browser. Complex search engines offer multiple different facets that control the type of results returned. For instance, one can search in a library catalog for the author *Toni Morrison* but then choose to filter results to only those bearing the "Literature—History and criticism" Library of Congress Subject Heading. Or perhaps one wants to see the most recently published results first rather than results sorted by their relevance to the search query. Modern search engines implement these filtering and sorting features by presenting the user with a checkbox or drop-down menu that, upon selection, updates the displayed results. Without JavaScript, the only way to update the display would be to reload the entire web page, a slow process that disorients the user. With JavaScript, one can dynamically update the displayed results, even incorporating new information from the web server, without the browser reloading the page.

Many libraries use JavaScript to record traffic to their web properties. While this in and of itself does not require programming knowledge, as most analytics solutions provide a simple snippet of code for you to paste in your website's markup, JavaScript can also record custom events that one defines. These events can be anything that JavaScript has access to, including what parts of a page users click on, how they interact with tabbed search interfaces, whether they play embedded videos, and more. There are many examples of libraries using this capability to discover user behavior that can in turn be used to improve user interfaces or demonstrate the popularity of a particular service. To name but two examples, Kirk Hess used custom events tracked with JavaScript and the colossally popular Google Analytics service to learn how visitors interacted with the University of Illinois at Urbana-Champaign's digital library (Hess 2012), and JavaScript was used to record usage data for the Summon discovery layer (Pattern 2012; Reidsma 2012).

Summon did not report the statistics that librarians were interested in, thus the need to resort to JavaScript. Libraries often subscribe to vendor web products that, while offering some custom options, do not provide finely grained controls for all of their functions. Librarians may be able to insert custom HTML in a particular section of the site but not turn off certain features or construct new ones. Luckily, if the vendor site does allow one to insert JavaScript (typically via a `<script>` tag in your custom HTML header or footer), the possibilities for customization are great. Since JavaScript is specifically made for modifying web pages, the vendor site can be modified in many ways: elements can be removed, text on the page can be altered, interactions specified by the vendor's JavaScript can be superseded, and custom features can be inserted. It is worth noting that all customization runs the risk of conflicting with an original feature or breaking when the vendor introduces changes in its site.

Multitab search boxes, filtering search results without a page refresh, recording custom analytics, and customizing vendor websites are but a few of the common uses of JavaScript in libraries. Data visualization, using data from third-party sources, personalization using information stored in cookies, and much more can be done. JavaScript is *the* programming language of the web, and the web's ubiquity makes it a powerful tool for almost any task.

While historically used almost exclusively in a web browser environment, recent projects have begun to add capabilities to JavaScript beyond the creation of dynamic HTML documents. Mozilla's Rhino project provides the means to embed JavaScript inside Java applications (Mozilla Developer

Network 2014). Rhino is used to make certain functions scriptable within the EQUELLA digital repository, for instance. While Rhino was one of the earlier projects to bring JavaScript outside the web browser, the introduction of Node.js in 2009 by Ryan Dahl played a significant role in expanding the uses of the language (Dahl 2009). Node.js adds the ability to perform web server and file system operations, allowing programmers to write fast web applications and command line tools. There are also projects, such as Apache Cordova, which allow one to write a native app using traditional web technologies (HTML, CSS, and JavaScript) instead of the typical Objective C or Java (Apache Software Foundation n.d.). Most recently, Apple has expanded the means of automating programs in its OS X desktop operating system from only its proprietary AppleScript language to include JavaScript as well (Apple 2014). While JavaScript once was only used in browsers, it can create server-side applications, native mobile apps, and desktop software. This flexibility means that the language is a competitor to popular, multipurpose interpreted languages, such as Python and Ruby.

PROS AND CONS

JavaScript's tremendous popularity is a boon, particularly for new coders. Since almost every problem has already been encountered when writing JavaScript, numerous answers, tutorials, and documentation exist online. Furthermore, there are many popular JavaScript libraries that solve common problems. These libraries can be employed to help you rapidly develop complex applications with very little of your own code. While many programming languages share a strong set of libraries and online assistance, JavaScript is among the best.

JavaScript is a flexible and forgiving language. Like many high-level scripting languages, it abstracts over the intricate minutia of dealing with computer hardware and worrying about memory allocation. One can write code without understanding how the underlying machine must handle it. On the whole, JavaScript tends toward lenience. Where other languages throw errors that stop a program in its tracks, JavaScript will continue while providing clues that something is wrong. An excellent example of this clemency is accessing object properties that do not yet exist; while many other languages throw a reference error in this situation, JavaScript returns "undefined." Instead of complicated error handling patterns, one can thus perform simple tests to see if a property exists. The language also has a flexible type system. Types are how different data are classified by programming languages, for instance, as integers, strings of text, or more complex objects with sets of special properties. JavaScript does not force one to declare a variable's type when it is created, does allow variables to change types during their lifespans, and does not force one to declare what types of data are allowed to be passed to one's functions.

The debate over whether strongly or weakly typed programming languages are superior is decades old. The debate will not be settled by this paragraph. Nonetheless, weak-type systems benefit beginning programmers. The beginner does not have to first accumulate exhaustive knowledge of a language's data structures before being able to use it. Furthermore, code written in weakly typed languages can create elegant interfaces that accept multiple data types and perform intuitive actions based on what is given. The enormously popular jQuery library, which will be covered later, takes wonderful advantage of this opportunity. For example, once you have selected an HTML element with jQuery, you can alter its appearance with the css method. This method can accept a pair of strings—the first being the property name and the second its value—to apply a style written in the Cascading Style Sheets (CSS) language to the element. But the css method also accepts an object of property-value pairings, allowing the programmer to set multiple styles at once. If JavaScript was strongly typed, css would only be able to accept *either* two strings *or* an object, making this intuitive interface impossible.

JavaScript's implementation of functions is particularly strong. The language treats functions as first-class objects, which means, essentially, that functions can be dynamically created, passed as parameters, or used in places where other languages limit the programmer to a static data type such as strings of text or numbers.

To demonstrate the power of JavaScript's functions, let's look at using functions as parameters. One can pass a function *to another function* as a parameter due to its first-class status. For instance, consider a function that does some data processing which can either complete successfully or encounter an error, perhaps due to being passed incorrectly formatted data initially. One can write a processData function that accepts two functions as parameters; one that is called if the processing is successful and given the now-processed data as a parameter, and one that is called if an error occurs that is given the error as a parameter. This provides enormous flexibility, since, rather than specifying error or success behavior within the processing function itself, these cases can be broken out into separate functions that can differ over the course of the program. One can call processData in one context with a very stringent error-handling function that causes the whole program to halt, and then call it again in another context where the user is notified of errors and given a chance to correct his or her input.

Passing functions as parameters to other functions is a common property of *asynchronous* programming. Asynchronous programs do not execute from top to bottom in the order they are written; rather, certain "events" can happen at any time and trigger corresponding code. *Asynchronous* programming patterns are common on the web and in interface design. In JavaScript, events include receiving data from another web server or user interaction, such as mouse movement. Every time information suddenly spills onto a web page without a refresh, for instance as a social network loads incoming posts, asynchronous JavaScript code is responsible.

Unfortunately, JavaScript is not a perfect programming language. Unlike other languages, where design choices may not suit everyone's taste but generally have a rationale behind them, JavaScript has flaws that even its creator acknowledges. Probably the most noticeable flaw in JavaScript is that all variables are, by default, global (Crockford 2008). The value of a global variable is its accessibility everywhere in a program, as opposed to local variables whose values are only available within limited scopes. Overuse of global variables causes bugs because disconnected pieces of a program may reuse the same variable name while expecting different values. In JavaScript, any variable declared without the `var` keyword is global. Global variables quickly lead to conflicts when multiple scripts by multiple authors are combined, as often happens on even relatively simple websites. For instance, both the jQuery and Prototype libraries create a global variable named $; if one wants to use both libraries on a page, one must take care to avoid conflicts, for instance, with jQuery's `noConflict` method (jQuery Foundation n.d.-e).

JavaScript's type system, while flexible, also contains nuances that make it difficult to work with. JavaScript's comparison operators can be classified as either double or triple equals. The double equals compare two variables' *values*, while the triple equals compare both their values *and their type*. If this seems obtuse, it is. The difference between `==` and `===` (and their companions `!=` and `!==`) is a source of confusion. Another common task in programming complicated by JavaScript's type system is determining what data type is stored in a particular variable. In JavaScript, how a variable obtained its current value can affect what type the language's `typeof` operator reports. For instance, a string literal declared like `var s = 'hi'` has `typeof ===` `'string'` while a string created with the `String` function like `var s = String('hi')` has `typeof === 'object'` even though for virtually all intents and purposes the two variables are equivalent. For this reason, it's best to use literals for strings, numbers, and regular expressions instead of JavaScript's corresponding `String`, `Number`, and `RegExp` constructor functions. On top of these issues, `typeof` reports `object` for arrays, whether they were initialized with the `Array` constructor or with a literal, making it difficult to detect that data type.

Since JavaScript's flaws are relatively well known, useful programs have arisen that "lint" your code by looking for common problems. These problems can vary from outright syntax errors to code that, while technically correct, can be misleading or cause unanticipated side effects. For instance, both of the flaws mentioned above can be mitigated by code linters that warn against the use of double equals or the built-in constructor functions. While Douglas Crockford's JSLint was the program that popularized JavaScript linters originally, nowadays JSHint is a superior option. JSHint is open source, boasts numerous configuration options, and comes in a number of flavors, such as code editor plug-ins and a command-line tool (JSHint n.d.). The language itself is also trying to address flaws in its design through introducing new features that either replace older, broken ones or assist programmers in writing safer code. Strict Mode, introduced in ECMAScript 5 in 2009, enforces stricter coding standards by turning poor practice into errors, while features like `Array.isArray` correct for the aforementioned problems with determining a variable's type (ECMA International 2011, 51, 123; Mozilla Developer Network n.d.).

ENVIRONMENT AND SETUP

The Document Object Model (DOM) is a way of visualizing and describing web pages and apps. In other words, it is an *abstraction* of a web page. This is the abstraction used to describe web pages and apps in the literature, and, more importantly, the particulars of this abstraction are used by browsers when they "interpret" the web code a developer writes. This function of a web browser is known as the DOM application programming interface (API) (World Wide Web Consortium n.d.). Through the DOM API, scripting languages like JavaScript have access to the contents of a web document. The DOM, simply put, describes a tree structure, with all of the contents in a web page forming a hierarchy of objects (or *nodes*). Everything in a web document, be it a header, a button, or an image, forms an object within the document. Some of these objects are part of other objects. A piece of text may, for instance, fall below the cell of a table in this hierarchy because that cell is where the text is located. To the DOM API, an object begins and ends with HTML markup tags.

A web page or app may look like a single unit, but it is normally built out of a number of parts that work together. The website that a user sees is built from this collection of languages and runs inside the web browser. In a sense, the web browser acts like a computer within a computer. This is known as the "client side" of web code, because the source code itself is actually running on the user's computer (the "client"). The three main languages that client-side web code is built from are HTML, CSS, and JavaScript. Each of these languages is supposed to do a particular job in the client. Because of the limitations of technology, staggered historical introduction of these languages, and sloppy web coding, these languages have been allowed to bleed into each other a little. However, by restricting them to the roles, or *scopes*, described here, developers will have a better chance of building solid pages and apps.

HTML, the oldest of these languages, is meant to tell the web browser *what objects in a web page are*. HTML markup tells the browser what in the page is a heading, what is a paragraph, and how the page is divided into logical sections.

CSS, on the other hand, is meant to tell browsers *what objects in a web page look like*. CSS is very powerful and very granular, allowing developers to set colors, fonts, sizes, and even visibility, based on any number of an object's properties. CSS can also be variable, with different colors set based on conditions (pseudoclasses), such as whether or not the mouse pointer is hovering over the object in question.

The subject of this chapter, JavaScript, is fundamentally different from HTML and CSS. JavaScript is meant to tell browsers *what objects in a web page do*. Unlike HTML, which is just a language for marking up objects, or CSS, which is just a language describing the appearance of those objects, JavaScript is an actual programming language. Using the powerful DOM API, JavaScript can manipulate any node in a web document. In the DOM, things that happen in or to a web document (*events*) are also objects. Because it employs an asynchronous programming paradigm, as noted earlier, JavaScript can listen for these events and act in response to them, or even modify the events themselves in a variety of ways. In recent years, HTML5 and CSS3 have provided exciting new ways for JavaScript to interact with the DOM, creating new opportunities but requiring a flexible approach to JavaScripting skills (Bengtson 2013).

Within its scope, JavaScript is extremely powerful; however, there are a number of things that JavaScript isn't allowed to do for security reasons. JavaScript, for instance, isn't allowed to save, modify, or in most cases even load files from your local computer. JavaScript can't send emails directly. JavaScript can't load data files, like XML, from any domain that is outside the web domain of the document it is within (Ruderman 2014). There are two exceptions to that last rule, but one has to be activated on a server and the other is an advanced technique called JSON-P that only works with data files in JavaScript Object Notation (JSON). JSON-P is a little beyond the level of scripting in this chapter. What is important for you to understand is that there are a number of actions that fall outside the scope of JavaScript but which may be effectively accomplished using server-side scripting with a language, such as PHP, Python, or Perl, which are all discussed in other chapters.

There are three basic ways to add JavaScript to a web document. The two fastest and easiest are also the two sloppiest: internal JavaScript and inline JavaScript. There is a time and a place to use both of these methods, especially when you have no choice but to be a little sloppy due to time constraints, but they produce lower-quality web code and may introduce unexpected problems into your app or page. The third and best method is to use an external JavaScript file. Besides creating a cleaner separation of JavaScript from HTML and CSS, external JavaScript files, like external CSS files, can be easily reused by multiple web documents. Additionally, using external Java-Script files forces creators to employ healthier techniques to handle events in the DOM, as we'll see later.

Internal JavaScript in a web document looks much like internal CSS. The script is placed inside `<script>` tags, like so:

```
<script>
document.getElementById('container').innerHTML="<p>This is
a paragraph</p>";
</script>
```

Inline JavaScript takes advantage of special tag attributes that allow you to put JavaScript right into an HTML tag so that the HTML object delineated by the tag can act based on events. The JavaScript that looks for an event is known as an *event listener*, while the JavaScript that acts in response to the event when it is detected is known as an *event handler*. Here is an example of some simple, inline JavaScript:

```
<a href="#" onclick="changeColor();">Click this link to
change the background color</a>
```

The `onclick` attribute calls the function `changeColor` if the link is clicked. The link's default behavior is handled by using # for the `href` attribute. In essence, we tell the link not to go anywhere when the user clicks on it. This probably seems temptingly straightforward. However, inline JavaScript has some inherent problems, as will be discussed further when jQuery event handlers are described.

Adding an external JavaScript file to a web document is easy. Essentially, it just involves a script tag that contains an `src` attribute pointing to a Java-Script file, like so:

```
<script type="text/JavaScript" src="js/combined.js">
</script>
```

jQuery

As previously noted, within its scope, JavaScript is extremely powerful. However, it can also be surprisingly unwieldy for simple tasks. Given that JavaScript is essentially the "wiring" that allows the elements in a web page to actually do useful things, and given that, in most cases, the things you will want your web code to do will be driven by the actions of your users (events), it is essential to "attach" your JavaScript to objects in a web page. Such attachments initiate JavaScript in response to user actions on those elements, such as when a user clicks on a button or tries to drag an image. Building these event handlers for elements in a web page with pure JavaScript, however, tends to be clunky. Let's say we have a button with the id push_this and we want to activate the function doSomething when a user clicks on it. To attach a click event to it in JavaScript, our code would look like this:

```
document.getElementById('push_this').
addEventListener('click', function() {doSomething();});
```

We could also just add the function to an onclick attribute in the button element itself (inline JavaScript), like so:

```
<button id="push_this" onclick="doSomething();">
```

However, this kind of event handling is sloppy and often leads to unanticipated consequences while producing web code that can be difficult to troubleshoot and rewrite. It is always best to avoid mixing script and markup languages together, since, as noted earlier, all JavaScript that runs in this fashion runs in what is known as the "global" scope. In other words, you can run into problems where multiple things you are trying to do with JavaScript interfere with each other because they are all part of the same scope.

This whole process can be improved by using a JavaScript library called jQuery. The jQuery library is free and can be downloaded from the web to be added to your site. jQuery is loaded into your page just like any other external JavaScript file, using a script tag:

```
<script type="text/JavaScript" src="jquery.js"></script>
```

There are also hosted copies of jQuery available online that you can reference instead of using a local copy. The advantage is that if those hosted copies are on a content distribution network (CDN), they may load into your page for end users more rapidly than if they reside on your servers with your web code. The down side is that you have no control over those hosted copies, or the servers they run on. This can lead to problems from unexpected outages or content servers being compromised. I have seen this happen at organizations, so I recommend using a local copy of libraries such as jQuery.

jQuery extends the power of JavaScript, making client-side scripting easier to do. Let's add our event handler to the button we saw previously using jQuery:

```
$("#push_this").click(function(){ doSomething(); });
```

This event handler is far more compact than the one we built in straight JavaScript, and it is more flexible and less likely to cause unanticipated problems than using the `onclick` attribute. Astute readers will also notice that, in selecting an element, jQuery uses CSS selector notation (`#push_this`). jQuery utilizes the "sizzle" selector engine, which leverages the extraordinary power of CSS selectors for use with scripting.

jQuery's handy ability to select objects in a web page with flexibility and precision and easily add event handlers to them is only part of its true power. jQuery also does an admirable job of dealing with issues of cross-browser compatibility (jQuery Foundation n.d.-c). That is to say, not all browsers always interpret JavaScript the same way. There may be slight differences in how they navigate the nodes in the Document Object Model (DOM) or how they allow JavaScript to interact with the DOM. jQuery is designed to cope with the nuances between browsers so that the end result of your script remains relatively consistent for your users.

In the same way that jQuery provides shorthand for selecting objects, jQuery also provides a wide variety of functions and *methods* (commands performed on an element in a web page) for web coders to use in order to more quickly accomplish both common and complex tasks. In a web document, for instance, objects can be moved around by setting their position or by changing their margin settings. With jQuery, however, you can simply use the `.animate()` method (jQuery Foundation n.d.-b). For AJAX, jQuery has a whole host of functions that smooth over inconsistent browser support and simplify the entire process, as shown in table 4.1 (jQuery Foundation n.d.-a). Everything from altering element attributes to making web document objects appear and disappear can be handled quickly and efficiently using jQuery methods. A few of the many jQuery methods are shown in table 4.1.

Table 4.1. Examples of jQuery Methods

Method	Description
`.hide()`	Sets an HTML element to display:none, causing it to disappear
`.show()`	Causes a hidden HTML element to be shown
`.attr()`	Find or change the value of an attribute of an HTML element
`.css()`	Find or change the CSS properties of an HTML element
`.each()`	Cycles through a collection of matched elements
`.val()`	Used to find or change the value of an HTML element
`.html()`	Sets the innerHTML value of an HTML element (allowing you to rewrite an element's HTML)
`.wrap()`	Wraps selected HTML elements with another element
`.bind()`	Add event handlers to an HTML element

Using these methods, we can simplify our JavaScript. Take this method for adding a class to an identified HTML object using straight JavaScript as an example:

```
document.getElementById("topHeader").setAttribute("class",
"green");
```

By employing jQuery, we can accomplish the same thing with jQuery selectors and methods:

```
$("#topHeader").attr("class", "green");
```

To simplify things even further, rather than using the generic `.attr` method, we can use the specialized `addClass` method, like so:

```
$("#topHeader").addClass("green");
```

Similarly, this cumbersome statement for making a div disappear:

```
document.getElementById("hideThis").setAttribute("style",
"display:none");
```

can be rewritten as:

```
$("#hideThis").hide();
```

To attach an event handler to an object in a web document, or to affect an object using a method, that object must be present in the web document. Such a statement may seem like a trite observation, but, in fact, it carries significant repercussions since browsers read a web document from top to bottom. In other words, you need to introduce your JavaScript methods into the web document after the objects they reference. That's why some developers have long insisted that, while most libraries like jQuery should be added in the head of a web document, other JavaScript should be added at the bottom, just before the closing body tag. jQuery has a much better way to handle this, however, using the .ready() function (jQuery Foundation n.d.-f).

You can enclose all of a web document's event handlers and methods in the .ready() function (which is attached as an event handler to the document object), like so:

```
$( document ).ready(function() {
 $("#push_this").click(function(){ doSomething(); });
});
```

Now the event handler won't be referenced until the framework of the document is in place, ensuring that the event handler has something to hook into. This is a very general way to use enclosing functions, known as closures, to control the scope of your JavaScript (Johns n.d.). Closures are a topic that needs more treatment than can be given here, but by controlling scope, rather than leaving your script in its default scope of global, it becomes easier to write clean JavaScript. Closures are one technique for dealing with the global scope default present in JavaScript.

jQuery makes writing JavaScript easier, improves cross-browser compatibility, and lends itself to higher-quality client-side script. The jQuery library is a powerful tool for anyone seeking to write high-quality JavaScript as painlessly as possible.

EXAMPLES

Here are a few simple scripts to get the reader started. In order to provide examples that can easily be typed directly into the reader's text editor and tested in a web browser, the JavaScript is shown here as internal (between script tags) rather than as a separate file. Readers may easily test these examples by typing them into a simple text editor, such as Notepad, saving them as a file with the .html file extension, and opening them in a web browser. Do not use a word processing program, such as Word or Pages, as these will add special characters to the web code that may keep it from functioning. These scripts may be copied and reused at the whim of the reader.

Add Two Numbers

This script creates two prompt boxes that each accept a number. The numbers are added together before the answer is outputted into an alert box. `parse-Float` is used when calling the prompt boxes to convert the strings (plain text characters) they normally capture into floating point numbers so they can be added up. Note the use of a function (`addThem`) that serves as a reusable block of code. Technically, any two numbers could be fed into `addThem` as parameters to generate an answer, including numbers that do not originate from the prompt boxes.

```
<!DOCTYPE html>
<html>
<head>
<meta http-equiv="Content-Type" content="text/html;
charset=UTF-8">
<title>Add Two Numbers</title>
</head>

<body>
<script>
function addThem(first, second)
{
     var answer=first+second;
     alert("the answer is: "+answer);
}

var first = parseFloat(prompt("Enter Your First Number",
0));
var second = parseFloat(prompt("Enter Your Second Number",
0));
addThem(first, second);
</script>
</body>
</html>
```

Say My Name

The following example uses a prompt box to accept a user's name before outputting a personalized message in an alert box. Once again, the script block uses a function, which accepts the name from the prompt box as a parameter. In this example, however, we are using the "string" that the user inputs as a string of text, and so we have no need to convert this input into numerical values as we did in the last example.

```
<!DOCTYPE html>
<html>
<head>
<meta http-equiv="Content-Type" content="text/html;
charset=UTF-8">
<title>Say My Name</title>
</head>
<body>
<script>
function myName(name)
{
     var message="Hello "+name+". We are sending you this
message from earth orbit. Do not adjust your television!";
     alert(message);
}

var name = prompt("Please Enter Your Name: ");
myName(name);
</script>
</body>
</html>
```

Redirect to a Mobile Site Based on Pixel Size

This simple script uses a combination of screen pixel width and information from the browser to send users to a mobile site if a mobile device is detected accessing the site. A real mobile site URL must be substituted for `http://www.google.com`. A number of interesting features are seen in this script. `screen.width` provides the "width" property of the "screen" object in pixels. `window.location.assign()` is one way to load a new web document from a specified URL. `navigator.userAgent` is a string of information about your device that is communicated to the browser. In this script we are searching this "user agent string" for "mob" to see if there is an indication in this string that the device is mobile as a backup to testing the size of the screen (especially important for high-resolution devices).

```
<!DOCTYPE html>
<html>
<head>
<meta http-equiv="Content-Type" content="text/html;
charset=UTF-8">
<title>Mobile Redirect</title>
</head>
<body>
<h1>This is the desktop Site</h1>
```

```
<p>Here is a paragraph of scintillating information</p>
<script>
if (screen.width <= 799 || navigator.userAgent.
indexOf('Mob') != -1)
{
     window.location.assign("http://www.google.com");
}
</script>
</body>
</html>
(Bengtson 2012b)
```

Change Link Destination for Mobile Device

This script uses a mechanism similar to the one above. Links that have the class `mobile` assigned, and which have a URL to a mobile-friendly alternate destination added as the `data-mobile` attribute in the HTML, will have the link destination switched if the script detects that a mobile device is accessing the site. This script requires jQuery. You should notice two interesting things about this piece of web code. First, we are loading jQuery into the web document via the first script tag from a Content Distribution Network. This is an example of loading an external JavaScript file, and it will work only on computers with Internet access. Secondly, unlike our other examples, here we are adding our JavasScript in the head of the web document. As discussed earlier, we can use the jQuery `ready` function to keep the event handlers from being attached until after the web document has been populated.

```
<!DOCTYPE html>
<html>
<head>
<meta http-equiv="Content-Type" content="text/html;
charset=UTF-8">
<title>Smartlinks Document</title>
<script src="https://code.jquery.com/jquery-2.1.4.min.
js"></script>
<script>
$(document).ready(function(){
     $("a.mobilev").click(function(e){
          e.preventDefault();
          var linkm=$(this).attr("data-mobile");
          var linkr=$(this).attr("href");
          mobileswitch(linkm, linkr);
     });
     function mobileswitch(linkm, linkr)
     {
```

```
        if ((screen.width <= 799)||(navigator.userAgent.
indexOf('Mobile') != -1))
        {
        window.location = linkm;
        }
        else
        {
            window.location = linkr;
        }
    }
});
</script>
</head>
<body>
<h1>This is the desktop Site</h1>
<p>Here is a paragraph of scintillating information</p>
<a class="mobilev" href="http://thenormaldestination.com"
data-mobile="http://themobiledestination.com">Here Is My
Link</a></body>
</html>
```
(Bengtson 2012a)

SUMMARY

JavaScript is the language that gives the web much of its dynamism, making it indispensable for libraries. Whether you need to spice up your website, create complex web apps to serve a variety of needs, or build web-based tools capable of communicating with data sources, JavaScript provides you with a flexible toolbox to help you accomplish your goals. As you build upon the basics in this chapter, keep in mind that the same programming structures and (as you become more cognizant of it) object orientation found in JavaScript will be present in other programming languages, including many of the other languages covered in this book. JavaScript offers a practical way to begin learning those skills.

BIBLIOGRAPHY

Apache Software Foundation. n.d. "Apache Cordova." https://cordova.apache.org/.
Apple. 2014. "JavaScript for Automation Release Notes." October 17. https://de
    veloper.apple.com/library/mac/releasenotes/InterapplicationCommunication/RN
    -JavaScriptForAutomation/index.html.

JavaScript 59

Bengtson, J. 2012a. "The Art of Redirection: One Library's Experiences and Statistical Results from the Deployment of Mobile Redirect Script." *Journal of Hospital Librarianship* 12 (3):191–98.

———. 2012b. "Scaling into the Future with Smartlinks." *Journal of Hospital Librarianship* 12 (4): 378–83.

———. 2013. "What Is HTML5 and What Do You Need to Know about It?" *Journal of Hospital Librarianship* 13 (4): 392–98.

Crockford, D. 2008. *JavaScript: The Good Parts.* 1st ed. Farnham, UK: O'Reilly Media.

Dahl, R. 2009. "Ryan Dahl: Original Node.js Presentation." November 8. https://www.youtube.com/watch?v=ztspvPYybIY.

ECMA International. 2011. *ECMAScript Language Specification.* Edition 5.1. Geneva: ECMA International. http://www.ecma-international.org/publications/files/ECMA-ST/Ecma-262.pdf.

ECMAScript Wiki. n.d. "People Working on TC39." http://tc39wiki.calculist.org/about/people/.

Flanagan, D. 2011. *JavaScript: The Definitive Guide.* 6th ed. Farnham, UK: O'Reilly Media.

Hess, K. 2012. "Discovering Digital Library User Behavior with Google Analytics." *Code4Lib Journal* 17. http://journal.code4lib.org/articles/6942.

Johns, M. n.d. "JavaScript Closures 101—They're Not Magic." http://www.javascriptkit.com/javatutors/closures.shtml.

jQuery Foundation. n.d.-a. "Ajax." http://api.jquery.com/category/ajax/.

———. n.d.-b. "animate()." http://api.jquery.com/animate/.

———. n.d.-c. "Browser Support." http://jquery.com/browser-support/.

———. n.d.-d. "jQuery API." http://api.jquery.com/.

———. n.d.-e. "jQuery.noConflict()." http://api.jquery.com/jQuery.noConflict/.

———. n.d.-f. ".ready()." http://api.jquery.com/ready/.

JSHint. n.d. "Documentation." http://jshint.com/docs/.

Mozilla Developer Network. n.d. "Strict Mode." https://developer.mozilla.org/en-US/docs/Web/JavaScript/Reference/Strict_mode.

———. 2014. "Rhino." April 14. https://developer.mozilla.org/en-US/docs/Mozilla/Projects/Rhino.

Pattern, D. 2012. "A Week on Summon." *Self Plagiarism Is Style.* May 12. http://www.daveyp.com/?p=1802.

Reidsma, M. 2012. "Guerrilla Analytics." July 30. http://matthew.reidsrow.com/articles/24.

Ruderman, J. 2014. "Same-Origin Policy." December 9. https://developer.mozilla.org/en-US/docs/Web/Security/Same-origin_policy.

Wood, C. M., B. Eich, J. Eames, A. Forst, A. J. O'Neal, J. Dance, and T. Caswell. 2014. "JavaScript Jabber 124: The Origin of JavaScript with Brendan Eich." September 3. https://devchat.tv/js-jabber/124-jsj-the-origin-of-javascript-with-brendan-eich.

World Wide Web Consortium. n.d. "Document Object Model (DOM)." http://www.w3.org/DOM/.

RECOMMENDED RESOURCES

GitHub phette23/js-chapter: https://github.com/phette23/js-chapter. A repository of short scripts written by one of the authors that demonstrates various concepts discussed in this chapter. Demonstrates some of the advantageous features of the language in simple, well-documented code.

HTML5 Rocks Tutorials: http://www.html5rocks.com/en/tutorials/?page=1. A suite of intermediate to advanced tutorials on new JavaScript APIs being introduced. HTML5 Rocks is a great place not only to learn about the latest features of the modern web but also to apply them right away.

JavaScript Mozilla Developer Network: https://developer.mozilla.org/en-US/docs/Web/JavaScript. Mozilla Developer Network (MDN) is perhaps the best source for readable documentation on the JavaScript language. MDN is the Wikipedia of web technologies: accessible, comprehensive, and filled with examples.

JavaScript Track, Codecademy: https://www.codecademy.com/learn/javascript. Codecademy provides online tutorials you can complete in your web browser. You will be assigned a task, write code to complete it, and then verify that your code works. There are tracks related to many important and major topics, such as jQuery and object-oriented programming.

jQuery API Documentation: http://api.jquery.com/. A resource almost as vital as MDN in terms of frequently consulted documentation. jQuery is a powerful and ubiquitous tool, and luckily its documentation is strong and full of examples.

Tizag JavaScript Tutorial: http://www.tizag.com/javascriptT/. An extended tutorial that walks you through many common applications of JavaScript on the web. Covers all of the major structural aspects of the language, from embedding a script in HTML to manipulating a dynamic web page.

Chapter Five

Perl

Roy Zimmer

HISTORY AND DEVELOPMENT

Perl was created in 1987 by Larry Wall. The design of Perl was influenced by Larry's background in linguistics, resulting in Perl's great flexibility. There are two acronyms associated with Perl: PERL itself, for Programmable Extraction and Reporting Language, reflecting its original intended use; and TMTOWTDI: There's More Than One Way To Do It. Perl is sometimes referred to as the Swiss Army knife of programming.

Perl was initially written to extract details from computer log files that system administrators have to look at. System administrators are the people who keep computers and their programs in good running order. Log files contain detailed records of the many things going on in a computer at any given moment.

There were several major releases of Perl in the years after 1987, "ending" with version 5 in 1994. Version 5 is still being updated, using a version number like 5.NN.n, with the more major updates incrementing the NN part. There is a version 6 of Perl, work on which started in 2000. Version 6 is, by design, considerably different from and independent of Perl 5, and, although you can use it, it is a work in progress. This chapter is only concerned with Perl 5, as that is what is commonly thought of as Perl. The correct way to refer to Perl is with only the leading *P* capitalized.

Perl was popular for coding web page interactions when the web was young, and some bad Perl code was written back then. This led to the misconception that Perl was a language to avoid. Well-written Perl code, like code written in pretty much any language, can be "beautiful code" that runs efficiently.

USES

Perl's wide adoption and continual updating lets you use it for just about anything on just about any kind of computer running almost any kind of operating system. Powerful enough for large and intensive computing needs, Perl was chosen early on for work with gene sequencing (https://web.stanford.edu/class/gene211/handouts/How_Perl_HGP.html). The BBC created an online database of over four million radio and TV programs dating back to the 1920s and, among other software, uses Perl on the web server (http://genome.ch.bbc.co.uk/). There is at least one major ILS that uses Perl behind the scenes, installing it with its product.

What can *you* do with Perl? Interact with databases, such as Oracle, MySQL, and Access. Customize how a web server handles interactions between users and web pages. Change the type of data stored in a file, say from comma-separated values (CSV) to tab delimited. Process images (pictures), manipulate and transform files, extract data from them. These are some examples of what you might want to do with Perl in a library setting.

PROS AND CONS

Perl is a scripting language, so the process of creating and running your program is relatively simple and quick. Given that there are typically multiple ways to do things in Perl, you may encounter code that is hard to read. In that case, look in a Perl book to gain the necessary understanding. Well-written Perl code should be understandable just from looking at it. Perl has a rich repository of code that anyone can incorporate into their programs. This is CPAN, the Comprehensive Perl Archive Network. Rather than reinventing the wheel for a particular task, take a look in CPAN first. The code in there is good; it is accepted only after being vetted by Perl experts.

One of Perl's strong suits is the use of the regex. This strange word is commonly used shorthand for a *regular expression*. Using a regex, you can search for a particular word, sequence of characters, or (most powerfully) a *pattern of characters*. Regexes can also be used to make substitutions or deletions. The origin of regular expressions goes back to neuroscience, logic, and computer science in the 1940s and 1950s. The arrival of Perl was one of the major forces behind making regular expressions widely understood among programmers.

EXAMPLE

Josie had a problem. Her library had a set of *Freddy the Pig* books that weren't cataloged well enough. A search for these didn't always show all the items. She wanted to fix this but didn't know how. Having an interest in computers beyond merely using them, Josie had experimented with Linux on her old laptop. She figured out how to extract and load a file of MARC bib records, working with her library's ILS, but that was as far as she got. She couldn't find a way to add a field to each of these records to make the collection correctly searchable. A friend of hers, Lisa, who wrote software for a living, had mentioned how much she liked using Perl, so Josie thought she'd give it a try. Between Lisa's willingness to help and Josie's explaining the structure of MARC records, they felt they could solve this problem. As any computer running Linux typically comes with Perl, and Josie's laptop had it, that was one hurdle out of the way.

Lisa mentioned, "If you wanted to do this on your Windows machine, that wouldn't be a problem. Installing Perl on Windows is easy." (See links at the end of this chapter.)

Working on Josie's Linux machine, Lisa had her get to the command prompt. In this chapter, the command prompt is shown as `>>` (your prompt may look different). Then, to double-check that Perl was installed, she had Josie enter the command `which perl`. Since the result from that was `/usr/bin/perl`, they were good to go. Otherwise, if the result had been just the command line prompt, Lisa would have had to install Perl for Josie.

Lisa decided to get Josie started with a simple program that says, "Hello, world." She had Josie use a text editor, enter the two lines below, and save it as hello.pl:

```
#!/usr/bin/perl
print "Hello, world\n";
```

One thing Josie learned was that, by default, any file or program you create has read-only permission. The file explicitly must be given file execute permission, allowing it to run. However, this is not true for Windows. Lisa showed her one way to do this:

```
>> chmod 755 hello.pl
```

and had Josie run the program:

```
>> perl hello.pl
```

It worked! This is what they saw:

```
>> Hello, world
>>
```

Let's examine `hello.pl`. Line 1 tells Linux where Perl is installed. Why? It is possible to have more than one version of Perl (or other programs) installed, and this line unambiguously indicates where to find it. That entire line is a comment for Perl, so Perl ignores it. The operating system, in this case Linux, "peeks" at the comment. This first line, or some variation of it, is required in Perl programs. If you use Windows, you can omit this line. Line 2 starts with the `print` function, followed by the double quotes surrounding the characters you want it to print. What's that \n at the end? That tells the print function to "move" to the beginning of the next line. You see the semicolon at the end of line 2? That tells Perl that line 2 is complete. Sometimes, when you have a long line of code, breaking it up into multiple lines makes it more readable. Perl knows it's the real end of the line when it encounters that semicolon. Note that there's more than one way to run a Perl program: `perl program.pl` or instead `./program.pl`.

Reading Data from a File

Lisa told Josie that she would now show her how to read a file using Perl, so Lisa first had her create a file called `testinput.file` and put several lines of text in it. The new program, called `fileio.pl`, appears below. The line numbers to the left are purely for reference; do not enter them in the program.

```
1  #!/usr/bin/perl
2  # fileio.pl
3  use strict;
4  use autodie;
5  my $infile = "testinput.file";
6  my $record;
7  open(INFILE, "<", $infile);
8  while ($record = <INFILE>)
9  {
10     print $record;
11 }
12 close(INFILE);
```

Josie created the program, and Lisa explained how it works. Line 1 we know about—it is a standard. Line 2 is a comment that contains the name of the program. It's good practice to have the name of the program as one of the first lines, usually with a short explanation of what the program does. Anything on a line after the # character is treated as a comment and is ignored by Perl. We'll see what lines 3 and 4 do in just a bit. Line 5 defines the name of the file to be read; it puts the file name that's inside the double quotes into the variable $infile. Simple variables are known in Perl as *scalars*, and they always have the $ as the first part of the variable name. Line 6 declares a variable but leaves it empty, that is, no data is initially stored in it. Line 7 prepares the file for reading. INFILE is the *file handle* (think of it as a connector between the program and a file) and should always be all uppercase.

The next part, <, specifies what we want to do with this file. Think of it as an arrow indicating in which direction the file data is moving; in this case, since we're reading the file, the data flows left from the file name to the file handle. In Line 8, we start the loop of file reading activity. $record = <INFILE> reads one line of the input file and puts that data into the variable $record. The file handle must be inside the < > angle brackets. This line starts with the word while, which requires a conditional statement, and that must be enclosed in parentheses. This doesn't look conditional, like *if such-and-such* . . . , that's true, but it is implied. When $record receives data, ($record = <INFILE>) is evaluated as being *true*. So line 8 says that while (or so long as) it is *true* that $record is getting data, do whatever comes inside the following curly brackets{ }. The curly brackets may contain any number of lines of code to be run. So long as we are successfully reading data, these lines of code will be run. When we reach the ending }, we return to the *while* part and try to read another line from the file. When the entire file has been read—that *while* condition evaluates as *false* (no more data)—we exit the loop and jump to the program line immediately after that ending }, line 12. We are done now and close the input file. The code inside the while loop is one line that prints our input file record to the screen.

But wait, we're forgetting something . . . or are we? Remember in the print statement in hello.pl, we had that \n at the end of what we printed? Why don't we have that here? When Perl reads a line, the \n is included from that file. Thus, we don't need to add it to the print statement.

Now let's cover lines 3 and 4. Whenever we see the construct use some_ module, we call in, or include, the program code of the specified module that resides somewhere else on your computer. Such modules contain a bunch of code that we can use (include) in our program, but we'll never actually see it (and do not need to). This keeps our programs simpler but gives them more power, as we can call on that module's functionality. So, what is use strict? Think of it as a proofreader for your program. It won't catch everything, but it will complain if you have syntax errors or make use of a variable without defining it. use strict is optional, but I recommend you always use it, as it will make your life easier. If you entered the program and ran it and didn't get any errors, great. Edit your program and comment out line 5 by putting a # at the beginning. Now run your program again. use strict will notice you have an undefined variable and will not let you run your program. Now also comment out line 3, eliminating that check, and try to run your program again. This time it will let you, but you'll get an error the moment you try to open INFILE, because there is now no file name.

use autodie is not required but is also highly recommended. Without that, if there's a problem interacting with a file (open, read, write, close), you will get a more helpful error message than you otherwise would. Note: If you get an error at line 4 when you try to run this program, you've got an older version of Perl that doesn't have autodie built in. In that case, comment out line 4 and the program should work.

Reading from One File and Writing to Another

Now Lisa had Josie modify the fileio.pl program. The changes are shown below:

```
1 #!/usr/bin/perl
2 # fileio.pl
3 use strict;
4 use autodie;
5 my $infile = "testinput.file";
6 my $outfile = "testoutput.file"; # new
7 my ($record, $linectr, $message); # new
8 open(OUTFILE, ">", $outfile); # new
9 open(INFILE, "<", $infile);
10 while ($record = <INFILE>)
11 {
12 print OUTFILE $record; # modified
13 $linectr++; # new
14 }
15 close(INFILE);
16 close(OUTFILE); # new
17 print "Copied $linectr". # two more new lines
18 "records from $infile to $outfile \n";
```

Line 6 doesn't show us anything new since it is a lot like line 5. Line 7 defines three variables. They are grouped inside parentheses, creating a list. The parentheses weren't needed before, when there was just that one item. It's more compact and still readable to declare multiple variables this way. Line 8 is new, and much like line 9, which we know from before. Note that the angle bracket > is now pointing right. That indicates our program will be writing to the file indicated by $outfile. Line 12 has changed. When you have print "this text", those two words will be echoed to your screen. That's because you didn't specify where to print, so *to the screen* is the default. We've put the file handle OUTFILE there, so this output will go only to the output file, $outfile. Line 13 is new. The ++ is an increment operator; every time we reach this line, 1 is added to $linectr. This is shorthand for $linectr = $linectr + 1. Recall that like $record, we defined $linectr but didn't provide a starting value. Thus $record starts out as an empty string " ", yet $linectr starts out as 0. Why is that? Context. When Perl sees that our first use of $record is for string values, it makes sure we start with $record = " ". Perl sees that our first use of $linectr is numeric, so it gives it a value of 0 before the program uses it. While this might seem confusing, it is much like spoken language. We often unconsciously determine a word's use or meaning from context—it just happens. This is one of the aspects of Perl that makes using it easier. If you want to make sure that a variable is a particular type, initialize it with the intended type of value.

Why are lines 12 and 13 indented? It makes it easier for us to see that these two lines are contained in the while loop. Indenting might not matter in a simple program like this, but in bigger and more complex programs, it really is a huge help. Perl doesn't care whether the lines are indented or not, but it's a habit we should adopt in our programs.

Line 16 shows us nothing new. Lines 17 and 18 are one line as far as Perl is concerned. It is broken up to show that you can do this and is usually done to make long lines of code more readable. You can, of course, ignore the comment in line 17—the code there ends with the . character. This is the string concatenation operator. It joins the string before it and the one following it together. You'll notice that the variable names are inside the string. Since we're using the double quotes around the strings, the values of the variables are substituted in that string. Were we instead to use single quotes around our strings, that value substitution would not occur; instead $somevariable is exactly what we would get, dollar sign and all.

When Josie ran the program, it showed that the same number of lines was copied as was in the input file. Lisa had her run the cat command for both the input and output files, and they could see that both files were identical. Success!

A Simple Regex Example

Lisa wanted to show Josie a simple example of using a regular expression, so she had her add this line to testinput.file, exactly as shown: Floyd was a `loyal` `man`. Then she had Josie change the code inside the `while` loop in `fileio.pl` so it looked like this:

```
{
    if ($record =~ m/loyal/) # new
    {
        print OUTFILE $record;
        $linectr++;
    }
}
```

There's a new line of code here that shows the `if` statement: *if (some condition)*. When the condition inside the parentheses ( ) evaluates as true, run the code inside the immediately following curly braces { }. This looks normal enough, but there are some strange characters there. The `=~` indicates a regular expression, or regex, follows. The / / characters surround the regex; the m in front means we're trying to match the regex with what's in `$record`. In this case, it is a simple regex that checks if the word *loyal* is in `$record`. Josie runs the program and sees that the only line copied to the output file is the line `Floyd` `is` `a` `loyal` `man`. as that's the only line in the input file with that word.

   "One more thing to show you is regex substitution," said Lisa and had Josie add one line before the print statement in `fileio.pl`:

```
$record =~ s/loy/FAP/;    # new
print OUTFILE $record;
```

When Josie ran the program now, there was again one line of output in `testoutput.file`, but it looked different: `FFAPd` `was` `a` `loyal` `man`.

   Josie figured out that the s that started off the regex meant substitution, replacing `loy` with `FAP`. But why was `loyal` still *loyal*, she asked Lisa.

   Lisa explained that only the first match would be substituted unless a g was at the end of the regex, for global (or all) matching substitution, in which case the regex would look like this: `s/loy/FAP/g`.

Reading a MARC File

Based on what Josie had told Lisa about the MARC file format, Lisa designed a program to read a MARC file and show the data in a human-readable format. Create a file called `marcread.pl` that looks like this:

```
1 #!/usr/bin/perl
2 # marcread.pl # provides human readable output for MARC
format file
```

```
3 use strict;
4 use autodie;
5 $/ = "\x1d"; # this character indicates the end of a
MARC record
6 my ($baseaddr, $strptr, $tagid, $taglen, $offset,
$tagdata);
7 my @marclines;
8 my $marcfile = "test.marc";
9 open(MARCFILE, $marcfile);
10 @marclines = <MARCFILE>; # read file all at once into
array of records
11 close(MARCFILE);
12 my $recnum = 0;
13 while ($recnum < @marclines)
14 {
15 printf("LDR:%s\n", substr($marclines[$recnum], 0, 24));
16 $baseaddr = substr($marclines[$recnum], 12, 5) - 1;
17 $strptr = 24;
18 while ($strptr < $baseaddr-1)
19 {
20 $tagid = substr($marclines[$recnum], $strptr, 3);
21 $taglen = substr($marclines[$recnum], $strptr+3, 4);
22 $offset = substr($marclines[$recnum], $strptr+7, 5);
23 $tagdata = substr($marclines[$recnum],
$baseaddr+$offset, $taglen);
24 # use " |x " for subfield delimiter where 'x' is the
subfield,
25 $tagdata =~ s/\x1f[a-z0-9]/ \|$& /g;
26 # remove original field and subfield delimiters
27 $tagdata =~ s/\x1f|\x1e//g;
28 # remove space before 1st subfield
29 $tagdata =~ s/^(..) \|/$1\|/;
30 # print a field and its data
31 printf("%3s:%4s:%5s:%s\n", $tagid, $taglen, $offset,
$tagdata);
32 $strptr+= 12;
33 }
34 $recnum++;
35 print "\n";
36 }
37 print "MARC records read: $recnum\n";
```

Notice that there are a few empty lines; these are useful to demarcate certain areas of a program and improve readability. Line 5 is new. Remember the concept of \n at the end of a line? That's standard for text files. The MARC format uses a different character, and Perl makes it easy to switch to that. In

Perl, there are certain two-letter reserved variables. One of them, $/, indicates what to use for the end-of-line marker; the default value is \n. In line 5, we're telling Perl to use the hexadecimal (base 16) value 1d (one d) instead. Perl knows it's a hexadecimal value because we put \x in front of it. Thus line 5 enables Perl to read MARC files like a regular text file.

In line 7, an array is being defined. In Perl, an array variable, when it's referring to the entire array, always has the @ in front of it. What is an array? It is a grouping of variables. Think of an encyclopedia with twenty-four volumes. That's an array of twenty-four books, having volumes 1, 5, 11, and so on. We could define an array as @encyclopedia. The fifth volume would be referred to in Perl as $encyclopedia[4], the eleventh volume as $encyclopedia[10], and so on.

"Wait a minute!" Josie exclaimed. "Why is volume 5 referred to as number 4 in the array?"

Lisa explained, "0 is a perfectly good number, and programmers decided to use 0 as the first element, instead of 1. It's not a Perl thing, as some other programming languages are like this also. It sort of makes sense, but it's confusing at the same time."

Josie thought for a second. "Ok. I guess I get that. But why is it $ency clopedia[4] instead of @encyclopedia[4]?"

"Remember, an array is a grouping of variables," Lisa said. "Variables always have the $ sign first in the name; that's how we know it's a variable. So you refer to $encyclopedia[n] to mean the *n*th variable (or volume in this example) in an array, well really *n*th + 1, whereas @encyclopedia refers to the array as a single unit, or the whole encyclopedia."

After thinking this over a bit, Josie indicated for Lisa to continue.

"Ok. Line 10 is where we put values into this array, and it's pretty cool, I think," Lisa went on. "Rather than the while loop we saw earlier, we can read the entire file all at once. Each variable, or element, in the array holds one line from the file we're reading. Unless you're reading a really huge file, this method works great! In line 12, we set up $recnum so that we can use it to refer to each record of elements in the array @marclines, and we set that up in the while loop in line 13."

"Wait, this is weird," Josie interrupted. "How can we compare a numerical variable to an array? That's like apples and oranges."

"Ah," Lisa answered, "context. Perl knows that $recnum is numeric, so it looks at array @marclines in a numeric way. How does it make that work? It knows the number of elements, or variables, in @marclines. So the while loop starts with $recnum as 0 and keeps accessing the variables in @marclines until it reaches element number *n*. However, element *n* does not exist since an array has elements 0 through $n-1$! At that point we're done with the `while` loop; no more data to process."

Lines 15–16 are mostly similar. Looking at line 16, we see that `substr` is the substring function, which curiously enough, copies a part of a string (of characters). From the record in array `@marclines` referred to by the current value of `$recnum`, extract a copy of the characters starting at position twelve for a total of five characters. Since we're extracting digit characters, and then doing math with them, the -1 part, Perl converts those five digits into one number and subtracts one, then puts that value into `$baseaddr`. Line 15 uses the print-with-formatting function to output the leader of a MARC record. The `printf` function has the formatting specified inside the double quotes. You can also put literal text in there, like `LDR:`, and also use characters like `\n`. Certain character groupings that start with `%` inside the double quotes signify a format. In this case it's a very basic `%s`, meaning it will handle a string of unspecified length and doesn't do any further formatting. After the double quotes is a comma, and the list of variables/values to be substituted inside the formats on the left. Here we have a single value, the result of that substring operation, which replaces the `%s` when `printf` does its thing.

The next line of interest is line 25. Yikes! Let's look at that regex one piece at a time. We know a substitution will occur since it starts with s. The first thing it looks for is a hexadecimal number. It is actually the unprintable character used to indicate or delimit a subfield in the MARC format. Then we look at what is inside the square brackets [ ], which indicates that we are looking for any lowercase letter or any single digit. Since that's how subfields are identified, we know that this regex looks for the start of a subfield. Now we have reached the / regex delimiter, so what follows is what we substitute *with*. That's a *space*, the | character, `$&`, and another *space*. The | character controls regex behavior (we'll show that later) and we want that actual character, so we *escape* it by putting the \ character in front of it. `$&` is one of those reserved Perl variables, and it contains what, if anything, was matched. And that's what we do in the first part of a s(ubstitution) regex; find or match something. An illustration helps with the above. In this example, let's show that subfield delimiter character, `\x1f`, using a ! to make things clearer. Example input: `!cPutnams`. Example output: `| !c Putnams`. This formatting is applied to all subfields, as the regex ends with g.

Line 27 may look a bit easier to understand. Here we are looking for the subfield and field delimiter characters and removing all of them. The | in that first part of the regex means match the `\x1f` *or* the `\x1e` character and remove these whenever encountered. Example input: `\| !c  Putnams`. Example output: `|c  Putnams`. Certainly more readable.

Line 29 removes the first space in a line only if it is followed by the | character. We know this one is doing substitution, since that s starts it off. The caret ^ (or hat) character means to start matching at the beginning. It looks for any two characters (indicated by the . .) at the beginning, then a *space*, and then the | character. Since we're looking for the actual | character, we have to escape it by putting the \ in front of it.

Josie is confused, "It sort of looks like that any-character part is going into $tagdata, but I'm not sure that's right. And where did that $1 come from? It's not part of the program."

"Excellent question," Lisa answered. "Any $n variables (where *n* is a single digit) are internal, or reserved, to regexes, and are used in that context."

So the characters matched by that (. .) in the left part of the regex are copied into $1. This regex carefully removes only the first space character. In another situation, this regex could probably have been simpler. Then we print out the processed current field's data in line 31. Here we have multiple formats in the left part of the printf function. The output for format %ns will always be a string that is n characters wide. The variables on the right are matched up in order with the formats on the left.

Now let's look at what we're doing from a MARC record point of view. If you are not familiar with the MARC format, visit the Library of Congress website at http://www.loc.gov/marc. The first twenty-four characters of a record constitute the leader, and we extract that as is. From within the leader, we extract the base address, the position in the record where the first field's data starts. In between that base address and the leader is the record's directory, consisting of twelve-character groupings for each field (245, 650, etc.) in the record. Each grouping specifies the field, how long it is, and how far after the base address in the record this field starts. Thus, after we get the leader and base address, we "loop" through the record's directory, grabbing each field's metadata and then its actual data. Then the subfield delimiters and transitions are formatted for easy readability and printed out.

Josie had the MARC file she'd created earlier, which she had called test.marc. As you try this example, you will need to create one on your own. For this example, it should be a small file of three or four records, bibs only, and also call it test.marc. When she ran marcread.pl, she could see the MARC records on the screen, now easily readable. Sample output: 082:0016:00367:04|a 617.9/6 |2 22. That's field *082*, length *16*, offset (from base address) of *367*, indicators *04*, and it has subfields *a* and *2*. We can actually make more use of this format. Let's redirect the marcread output to a file—we can do this without editing the program, like this: perl marcread.pl > test.read. This also works in Windows. Now, rather than seeing the output, we get nothing on screen and it all goes into file test.read. If we do not use the > to redirect the output, we'd see the results on screen again.

Looking at this output, Josie thought out loud, "Hmm, I'm using a text editor to look at this file, test.read. I know I could edit what I see, but is there any way of getting my changes into a MARC file?"

Lisa was happy to respond, "Yes! I've created a rudimentary program to do just that! It doesn't do any error checking, so if you're breaking some MARC rule, you're on your own. I called it marcunread.pl." Here it is:

```perl
1 #!/usr/bin/perl
2 # marcunread.pl works only with BIB records
3 use strict;
4 use autodie;
5 my $infile = "test.read";
6 my $outfile = "test.unread";
7
8 my ($line, $leader, $tag, $tagsize, $tagcontents,
$newrec);
9 my $recctr = 0;
10 my (@tags, @tagdata, @taglen);
11
12 my $subfdelim = "\x1f"; # MARC subfield delimiter
character
13 my $fdelim = "\x1e"; # MARC field delimiter character
14 my $recdelim = "\x1d"; # MARC end-of-record character
15 open(OUTFILE, ">", $outfile);
16 open(INFILE, "<", $infile);
17 while ($line = <INFILE>)
18 {
19 handledataline();
20 # last line in marcread format says: MARC records read: N
21 if (($line ne '') and ($line !~ /^MARC/))
22 {
23 $leader = substr($line, 4);
24 $line = <INFILE>;
25 handledataline();
26 }
27
28 # after the leader, get the rest of the record
29 while (($line ne '') and ($line !~ /^MARC/))
30 {
31 ($tag, $tagcontents) = ($line =~ /^(\d{3}).{12}(.+)/);
32 # undo subfield readability formatting; also perform
indicator check
33 if ($tag ge '010')
```

```perl
34 {
35 $tagcontents = substr($tagcontents, 0, 2) . $subfdelim .
36 substr($tagcontents, 3, 1) . substr($tagcontents, 5);
37 $tagcontents =~ s/ \|(.) /$subfdelim$1/g;
38 }
39 $tagsize = length($tagcontents) + 1;
40
41 # accumulate this record's data
42 push @tags, $tag;
43 push @tagdata, $tagcontents;
44 push @taglen, $tagsize;
45 $line = <INFILE>;
46 handledataline();
47 }
48
49 # if at end of logical MARC record write it out
50 if ($line eq '')
51 {
52 $newrec = createnewrec($leader, \@tags, \@taglen, \@
tagdata);
53 print OUTFILE $newrec;
54 @tags = @taglen = @tagdata = ();
55 }
56 if ($line =~ /^MARC/) {last;} # we *are* done
57 }
58 close(INFILE);
59 close(OUTFILE);
60
61 sub handledataline()
62 {
63 chomp $line;
64 $line =~ s/\t|\n|\f|\r//g;      # remove problematic
characters
65 $recctr++;
66 }
67
68 sub createnewrec()
69 {
70 my ($leader, $tagid_array, $taglen_array, $tagdata_
array) = @_;
71 my @tagids = @$tagid_array;
72 my @taglens = @$taglen_array;
73 my @tagdata = @$tagdata_array;
74 my @offsets;
75 my ($newmarcrec, $directory, $baseaddress, $idx,
$reclen);
76 my $offset = 0;
```

```
77
78 # data starts after leader and tags directory
79 $baseaddress = 24 + (scalar(@tagids) * 12) + 1;
80 # create the data directory, and the record; get the
record length
81 for ($idx=0; $idx<@tagids; $idx++)
82 {
83 $offset += $taglens[$idx-1] unless ($idx == 0);
84 $directory .= sprintf("%3.3d%4.4d%5.5d", $tagids[$idx],
$taglens[$idx], $offset);
85 }
86 $newmarcrec = $leader . $directory;
87 for ($idx=0; $idx<@tagids; $idx++) {$newmarcrec .=
$fdelim . $tagdata[$idx];}
88 $newmarcrec .= $fdelim . $recdelim;
89 $reclen = length($newmarcrec);
90 # update the leader; exit and return the newly built
MARC record
91 substr($newmarcrec, 0, 5) = sprintf("%5.5d", $reclen);
92 substr($newmarcrec, 12, 5) = sprintf("%5.5d",
$baseaddress);
93 return $newmarcrec;
94 }
```

"Wow, a bunch of new stuff here!" Josie remarked.

Lisa started explaining. In line 17, we're reading a line from the input file. Because of the logical sequence of how things happen in this program, we'll be reading a line from the file in several places. There are several things we do each time we read a line in. To keep the program shorter and more readable, those steps have been moved to a subroutine, handledataline, located further on in the program. Then, each time we need that functionality, there is just one line, which calls handledataline, instead of several lines to accomplish the same thing. The parentheses ( ) at the end of handledataline indicate that it is a subroutine. When the code in the subroutine has run, the program continues running at the next line after the call to the subroutine, line 21 in this case (line 20 is all comment). Line 21 is an *if* statement with multiple conditions. The use of parentheses helps to group them as intended. Since *and* is used, both conditions need to be true for the entire *if* statement to be true and the code in the following curly brackets { } to be run.

In line 23, the MARC record leader is copied into $leader, starting with the character at position four all the way to the end of $line. In other words, copy $line, except for positions zero through three. Then move on to the next input line by reading and preprocessing it. The *while* statement on line 29 makes sure that this line has data in it, as does line 21.

Line 31 looks intimidating, but let's figure it out. On the left is a list of two variables. The following equal sign, =, means we're assigning values to them from the regex.

"Wait a minute!" Josie interrupted. "I thought regexes resulted in a true or false value. And there's no m or s in front."

"True," Lisa continued.

When there's no letter in front of a regex, the m for matching is the default. Carefully looking at that regex, you can see two pairs of parentheses, ( ). Anything that matches the pattern inside them gets copied out. The result of the first pair gets stored in $tag, and the second goes into $tagcontents. With the caret or ^ we start matching at the very first position of $line. The \d by itself means to look for a single digit. The {3} right after overrides that a bit; it says to look for three digits. Since this looking-for-digits part is inside the parentheses, whatever matches goes into $tag. We know the . (dot) matches any character, but in this case, it's the next twelve characters, due to the {12}. In the second pair of parentheses, the + means one or more, so here we are saying that we don't care how many characters, nor which ones, so long as there is at least one. Since this part is inside the ( ), we put the remainder of $line, after the first fifteen characters, into $tagcontents.

Lines 35 and 36 are seen by Perl as one line, and there's nothing new there. The only new thing in line 37 is that there is a program variable in the regex, $subfdelim. This line is where the readable subfield formatting is changed back to the MARC format. Since the regex ends with the g, we will apply this transformation to all such format sequences in $tagcontent. Whenever there's a *space*, a |, any single character, and another *space*, keep only that single character that identifies the subfield and put the MARC subfield delimiter character in front of it. In lines 42–44, we are taking the variable on the right and making it the new *last* element in the array on the left, pushing it to the end, so to speak.

Skipping ahead a bit to line 54, we are making sure that each of those arrays are now empty and can be reused. Then, in lines 61–66, we see the simplest form of a subroutine. Basically, it's a named block of code, inside the { }, that we can use at will from elsewhere in the program. Each time that is done, those lines of code are run, and the program continues with the next line of code after where the subroutine is called. And what does subroutine handledataline do? Line 63 has chomp, which is new to us. It's commonly used, like here, to remove that \n from the end of a line. Additionally, in line 64, that and several other characters are removed from wherever they might occur in $line. That's \t for the tab character, our friend \n the line feed character, \f for the form feed character, and \r for the carriage return character. These are characters we do not want in a MARC record. If this regex finds *any* of these (there's the g for global at the end), it replaces them with nothing, effectively deleting them.

Now let's go back to line 52 and explain what it does. Subroutine creat-enewrec is called here; also, some data is sent to it, and it sends some data back. Specifically, it receives the leader data, all the field identifiers (245, etc.), each field's length, and each field's data. createnewrec assembles this data into a MARC record, which it sends back, or returns, to where it was called. In order for a subroutine to correctly receive an array, the array name should have a \ in front of it, in the call to the subroutine.

In line 70, we *receive* the data items that were sent to createnewrec. When a subroutine receives data items, they are all inside a single special variable called @_ and have to be separated out.

Josie was forced to interrupt: "Arrays were passed in but now they're variables?"

"That's kind of right," Lisa explained. "Think of it as a sort of file handle. Notice that in lines 71–73, we make sure we can refer to them as arrays like we normally do. It is one way of handling this to make life easier."

Line 83 is somewhat English-like, for program code. As long as the part to the right of the word *unless* evaluates as *false*, do what's to the left. The += operator adds what is to its right to the variable on its left. As you can see, you can put an expression inside the square brackets, [ ], used to refer to *array element n*, so long as the expression results in an integer.

Lisa showed Josie that she can check the syntax of a Perl program before running it: perl -cw program.pl.

Josie did so and corrected several typos, as indicated. Then she edited the test.read file, inserting a 650 field to enable better search results. Since this is in the marcread format, Lisa had her do it like this: 650:1111:11111: 0|aFreddie the Pig (Fictitious character) |v Fiction.

Those ones after the 650 are placeholders with meaningless values; mar-cunread.pl will figure out the length and offset for that field when it converts the data back to MARC format. Josie ran marcunread.pl and imported the resulting MARC file. She tried a search and success! She can now find all of these books with one search. Did anyone see the mistake I made in this program? It does not prevent the program from running correctly. Hint: It involves $recctr.

FINAL NOTES

In order to present these programs simply and compactly, they were shown in a stripped-down fashion. The use of more blank lines to set off sections of your code to make understanding it easier is encouraged. Also, error checking was omitted, particularly from `marcunread.pl`. A more complete version of that and other programs can be found at the author's web pages (http://homepages.wmich.edu/~zimmer/marc_index.html). All links shown below are current as of December 2015.

SUMMARY

Start out with simple Perl programs, working your way up to more complex programs as your skill set grows, at your own speed. Perl can implicitly handle programming details for you, letting you concentrate on the task you are trying to achieve. Programs can be written in a style where the functionality is obvious and readable, or dense and compact. The examples in this chapter show how to work with MARC data, doing all the "heavy lifting" yourself. Or you could choose from dozens of MARC-related modules on CPAN to make your task easier. You can do just about anything with Perl. Chances are good someone has written a module that will make your task easier.

RECOMMENDED RESOURCES

Websites

Get Perl, Command Line Version: http://www.activestate.com/activeperl/downloads; http://strawberryperl.com/.
Get Perl, Graphical User Interface: https://sourceforge.net/projects/citrusperl/files/.
Module Repository, CPAN: http://www.cpan.org/.

Books

Christiansen, Tom, Brian D. Foy, Larry Wall, and Jon Orwant. 2012. *Programming Perl: Unmatched Power for Text Processing and Scripting*. 4th ed. Sebastopol, CA: O'Reilly Media.
Christiansen, Tom, and Nathan Torkington. 2003. *Perl Cookbook*. 2nd ed. Sebastopol, CA: O'Reilly Media.
Schwartz, Randal L., and Brian D. Foy. 2011. *Learning Perl*. 6th ed. Sebastopol, CA: O'Reilly Media.
Siever, Ellen, Stephen Spainhour, and Nathan Patwardhan. 2002. *Perl in a Nutshell: A Desktop Quick Reference*. 2nd ed. Sebastopol, CA: O'Reilly Media.

Author's Links

MARC Programs: http://homepages.wmich.edu/~zimmer/marc_index.html.
Perl Stuff: http://homepages.wmich.edu/~zimmer/links/proglang.html#perl.

Chapter Six

PHP

Jason Steelman

HISTORY AND DEVELOPMENT

PHP is a beautiful, deceptively simple language. Its strengths are demonstrated ubiquity, platform conformity, ease of access, and the richest open-source community of any programming language. Most commonly, PHP works within a server to connect web pages to databases and perform the heavy lifting of web page manipulation; however, PHP can function as a stand-alone program. It is not uncommon to find free extensions that allow PHP to manipulate videos, data mine the web, or serve as the backbone of a site's content management system (http://php.net/manual/en/extensions .alphabetical.php). While many programming languages are chosen for their scalpel-specific features, such as task performance, hardware support, or high-level functionality, PHP is the sledgehammer capable of solving an epic score of problems—perhaps in a less elegant manner.

The bottom line for most library discussions on the acquisition of new software is cost. PHP's ubiquity and its open-source license mean that the language is almost always on the list of available options for a library. An important consideration in favor of PHP is the long-term support of a project offered by the language's battalions of developers. Finding a new developer largely depends on the complexity of the application's language. PHP developers are generally more affordable and more easily available to contract or employ compared to more robust languages. If the project lends itself to a complex program, there may be some additional time and initial cost to using PHP; however, long-term support for PHP projects is often more affordable. Compared to a corporation of similar scale, it is unusual for a library to require a new application within a relatively short time frame. With a flexible deadline, libraries can take advantage of the lower cost of PHP development as long as PHP is capable of solving the problem.

PHP's fit in a library's website can be difficult to pinpoint as it can be attributed responsibility for tasks in an application that it has not performed. PHP is not usually responsible for the literal storage of data, nor is it usually responsible for the visual display of a web page. PHP's usual responsibility on a website is to find data in a database or file system, run some calculations on that data, and send the data to the user. The calculation PHP is asked to perform is defined by a PHP script written by a programmer. The calculation can be as simplistic as "calculate the tax for this order" or as complex as "determine if this user has access to our top-secret files." PHP is not responsible for knowing the tax rate, nor is it responsible for knowing the order details. It must request the order details and tax rate from a database in order to make the requested calculation. PHP does not control how an order summary appears visually to the user as that is the role of the user's browser in conjunction with HTML, CSS, images, and JavaScript. Since PHP has well-defined scripts for getting data, running calculations on that data, and returning the results, PHP is often a simple way for a website to show raw data, such as a list of retail prices for books. Whether displaying raw or processed data, websites that need to show users information from a database commonly rely on PHP.

The evolution of the web correlates closely with the evolution of PHP. The first version of PHP was used as a tool to update one's "personal home page," PHP's original namesake. The robustness of PHP as a server language intended to run a single page was appropriate as websites during this time included blinking marquee text and animated GIF torches. The early web did not require complex pipelines to big data or mobile-compatible e-commerce. PHP had no reason to provide those features. As web developers began to expand our expectations for websites, PHP developed with advances in the web. PHP was renamed to stand for PHP: Hypertext Preprocessor and began to support the features a modern web programmer desires.

This slow evolution has left scars on the PHP language, including inconsistent naming conventions, strange required ordering of code, and legacy support issues. Consider the function names that ask if a variable is defined (isset), is an integer (is_int), or is a public variable (isPublic). Since PHP is case sensitive, a developer must either memorize the correct spelling for all functions or have a PHP manual at the ready. Modern coding tools help mitigate this issue with code completion, which acts like an automatic spell-check for programmers, but function names can make an introduction to PHP unnecessarily annoying. The best source for PHP documentation is php.net.

The advantage of its slow evolution is PHP's thoughtful inclusion of rich features and a variety of development environments. Programmers also have access to PECL (PHP Extension Community Library), which includes free PHP plug-ins that extend support for caching, compression, database connections, image manipulation, email, debugging, encryption, internationalization, and more.

ENVIRONMENT AND SETUP

The physical components (hardware) and programs (software) required before you can start working with a programming language are known as a development environment; however, your home and work computers are likely fully capable of developing PHP programs. Any website requires significantly higher hardware for a live web application, but a PHP programmer can develop and test applications on any normal workstation. The power required to run a live PHP program varies by the scale of the audience.

The most common installation of PHP for a production environment uses a series of programs that an average computer user will find foreign; however, it is common enough in server administration to earn an acronym, LAMP. Each letter in LAMP stands for a program: Linux, Apache, MySQL, and PHP. The most significant difference between the testing environment we will setup to write PHP versus our hypothetical production environment is Linux. Linux is the server's version of Windows and Apple OS. As the software that runs a personal computer, Windows and Apple OS are intended to provide a visual way of using and maintaining a computer with visual alerts when some program needs the user's attention. Web servers do not need a visual environment for alerts because servers are designed to run without the need for constant oversight. Linux intentionally excludes the types of software that make a personal computer personal in exchange for added power, stability, and security.

In order to test scripts in a way that replicates what will happen on a web server, a programmer tries to replicate the production environment on the testing computer as closely as possible. While learning PHP, there is no emphasis on creating a perfect, or even good, testing environment. As long as PHP can process scripts the developer needs processed and it ignores non-script content, the environment can be used for tutorials. The easiest way to designate a file or section of a file as a PHP script is to use encapsulating tags much like HTML itself:

```
<p>
    <?php echo "Hello World!"; ?>
</p>
```

In this example, the only portion of code sent to PHP is the command `echo` `"Hello World!"`. When a browser views this page, it will see something like `<p>Hello World!</p>`. There are other ways of distinguishing HTML from PHP, such as excluding the letters *php* (`<? echo "I'm missing the php letters, but why?"; ?>`), which is technically allowed but is inconsistent with today's best practices.

PHP is inherently inconsistent, and there are some areas where developers can help by agreeing to use one method where multiple methods may exist. Collectively, these agreements are known as best practices or coding standards. The majority of best practices are commonsense guidelines, but some content management systems, including Drupal and WordPress, add additional best practices when working with those systems. Projects built with PHP often have carefully considered best practices for that system. Drupal, being the largest of these projects, has established guidelines that have seeped into the general PHP developer universe. Guidelines on documentation are an important best practice from Drupal's impact but were not born out of Drupal but, rather, standardized. Code organization, file organization, and folder structure have little to do with coding itself, but a unified way of organizing projects makes group work far easier. Organizing your code and files in a way that is consistent with best practices ensures that co-workers, community developers, and future developers can quickly understand your code. Nonframework-specific standards represent efforts to create interoperable PHP best practices. The most notable nonframework standard is PSR-1, from the PHP Standards Recommendations from PHP-FIG (http://www.php-fig.org/psr/psr-1/), which is a democratically approved and voluntarily utilized set of standards.

PHP Applications for a Library

The predominant programming language used in library software is PHP. Drupal, ContentDM, Joomla, ResourceSpace, WordPress, LibGuides, MediaWiki, and PHPMyAdmin are written entirely or partly with PHP. It is common for a PHP application to include HTML, CSS, and JavaScript for visually pleasing websites. Any customizations a library needs to perform on these systems not covered in an initial installation or support contract must be made by a PHP developer. Drupal, WordPress, Joomla, and MediaWiki are open-source projects that are focused on expandability, with modular extensions that can be contributed by the developer community. The inspirational idea behind modular extensions is that no institution or library is an island; likewise, any feature a librarian might write to help patrons can help any number of other libraries' patrons. Employees who work within institutions should check to ensure their institution's intellectual property policies coincide with their position working on open-source projects.

Modern websites have taken on features developed for mobile sites, which feel more like web apps with very responsive designs. This is frequently made possible with JavaScript talking to an application program interface (API) powered by PHP. An API gives browsers ways of communicating with a server when other mechanisms are not feasible. PHP can generate data that is sent to a browser when a user requests a web page; however, once that page has loaded, PHP cannot change any part of the page. Instead, the page includes JavaScript that updates sections of a page with new data by asking an API for an update. Users can find live weather updates, election results, shipping statuses, and updated social media posts without having to refresh their page. It is important to note that PHP is not the only language capable of creating an API; however, it is a popular choice in library environments.

PHP is a common choice for API programming languages because PHP has documented ease of communication with databases. PHP can communicate with CUBRID, DB++, dBase, filePro, Firebird/InterBase, FrontBase, IMB DB2, Informix, Ingres, MaxDB, MongoDB, mSQL, Mssql, MySQL, Oracle OCI8, Paradox, PostgreSQL, SQLite, SQLite3, SQLSRV, Sybase, and tokyo_tyrant (http://php.net/manual/en/refs.database.vendors.php). Support for advanced database features in a PHP application ultimately varies based on the specific database used in the application. Where a chosen database lacks support for a certain feature, PHP can sometimes accommodate.

PHP Basics

Handling information going to and returning from databases is the role of variables. Variables are the core of any programming language, and PHP's way of handling variables is one of the areas weakened by its history. Where other languages explicitly define a variable as a number or word, variables in PHP do not have strict data types. From the perspective of a seasoned PHP developer, required data type definitions seem like an annoying hurdle. A lack of stated data types can cause problems while learning the language, especially when it comes to making an application more efficient. If your application has a series of true/false variables, storing that in memory the same way you would store whole textbooks would waste precious memory. PHP tries to allocate enough memory for each chunk of data without overtaxing the system. Working with databases poses interesting issues considering that most databases explicitly define each piece of data. Careful consideration is needed when sending data to a database to be stored. Retrieving data from a database is less traumatic because it is easier to move data from a more specific container to a less specific container. Likewise, it is easier to convert an on/off switch into words than words into whether a switch is on or off.

Libraries and special collections have a growing interest in encoded archival documents. The nature of an electronic thesis or dissertation (ETD) suggests that each field be carefully considered for a certain type of data. That precision can be lost if not preserved within the application itself. Languages that support data types require the type of variable (number, string, true/false, date, and similar), which has a clear advantage when working with ETDs. PHP developers could view these data-type considerations as a bit unnecessary, if only because there is not a clear way to keep track of variable types in the PHP language.

String, integer, floating point number, array, Boolean, objects, and resource are the seven types of data PHP can store as variables. Variables are defined in PHP using a dollar sign followed by the name of the variable you want to create or change. For example, $my_variable = 123.

- A *string* is a sequence of numbers or characters. Letters, words, sentences, paragraphs, and books can be stored as a string: $my_variable = "Go Gamecocks!".
- An *integer* is a whole number: $my_variable = 2.
- A *floating point number*, sometimes called double precision number or float, is a fractional number: $my_variable = 3.14159.
- An *array* is a variable that is a collection of other variables. Its form can be a little confusing to see for the first time and its true usefulness is beyond the scope of this introduction, but, like all PHP topics, there's no shortage of free tutorials: $my_variable = array("Cat", "Dog", 2, 4, 6, 8).
- A *Boolean variable* holds a binary value of true or false. This datatype has a wide variety of uses, such as on/off, yes/no, dog/not-dog, checked-in/checked-out, clean/dirty: $book_checked_out = true.
- *Objects* are a type of variable that are like subroutines that can hold their own code and variables internally. Objects are discussed in the section on object-oriented programming in PHP: $my_object = new my_object().
- *Resources* are objects that connect PHP to additional resources like databases: $my_connection = new database_connection().

Variable names have some minor rules and some additional best practices. This outline of do-nots can look overly restrictive but, in practice, makes variables more identifiable:

- Variable names must only contain uppercase and lowercase letters, numbers, and underscores: $this!sn0tV@lid.

- They cannot start with a number: `$2bad`.
- (Best Practice) Names should describe what they do. `$time_event_ starts = "2020-05-29"`.
- (Best Practice) Names should not start with an underscore: `$_gener- ally_bad`.

For learning and debugging purposes, these instructions will outline a standard Windows environment. These instructions depend on two downloads for NetBeans and WampServer. NetBeans will be used as our integrated development environment (IDE). An IDE can identify missing characters, provide code completion, and aid file management. WampServer (Wamp stands for Windows, Apache, MySQL, and PHP) will serve as the production environment that will process PHP code written in NetBeans and display the results in a browser. WampServer requires certain network permissions to run correctly because it causes your computer to act as a web server. These instructions can be modified for Macintosh computers by replacing WampServer with MAMP (http://www.mamp.info/en/). If you have already installed NetBeans for working with other languages, you can add support for PHP by installing the PHP plug-in from within the NetBeans plug-in tool.

- Download WampServer from http://www.wampserver.com/en/. If you are unsure if you need the 32-bit or 64-bit version, use the 32-bit option.
- Install WampServer using the default install location: `C:\Wamp`.
- Allow WampServer to start after the install has finished. Whenever there is new code to test, WampServer will need to be running.
- By default, you should now be able to visit http://localhost in your favorite web browser. If you get an error about connecting to the server, there is a problem with the WampServer installation.
- Download NetBeans with HTML5 and PHP from https://netbeans.org/ downloads/.
- Install NetBeans. There are no options during the NetBeans installation that affect this tutorial.

To create a project that can be authored in NetBeans and tested by WampServer, these programs need to be set up to operate on the same files. WampServer's default folder location is `C:\Wamp\www\`, which should be empty at this point. The test project will be called `my_project`.

- Create a folder in `C:\Wamp\www` named `my_project`.
  - Select Start > Computer.
  - Select `Local Disk (C:\)`.
  - Select the `Wamp` folder.

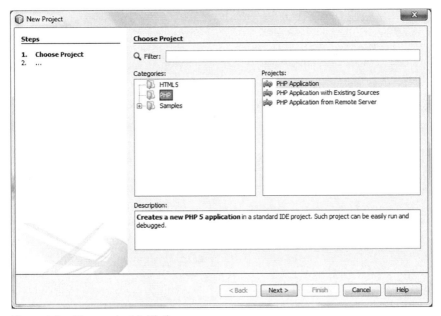

Figure 6.1.   New project initiation.

- Click New Folder at the top of the screen.
- Type my_project as the folder name.
- Launch NetBeans.
- Select File >New Project.
- Under the project category section, select PHP, then PHP Application under Projects (figure 6.1).
- Click Next.
- Name the project my_project (project names can have spaces, but consistency never hurts) and set the Sources folder by browsing to the newly created my_project folder at C:\Wamp\www\my_project\ (figure 6.2).
- Leave the PHP Version, Default Encoding, and Metadata folders to their default values and click Next.
- The Run Configuration window defines how the project should be deployed. When testing a project on a server, the remote settings allow NetBeans to directly upload and download from the server. For testing, debugging, and offline development, select Run As Local Web Site. Use http://localhost/my_project/ as the Project URL if it is not already entered (figure 6.3).
- Frameworks and Composer inclusions are beyond the scope of this tutorial. Select Finish.

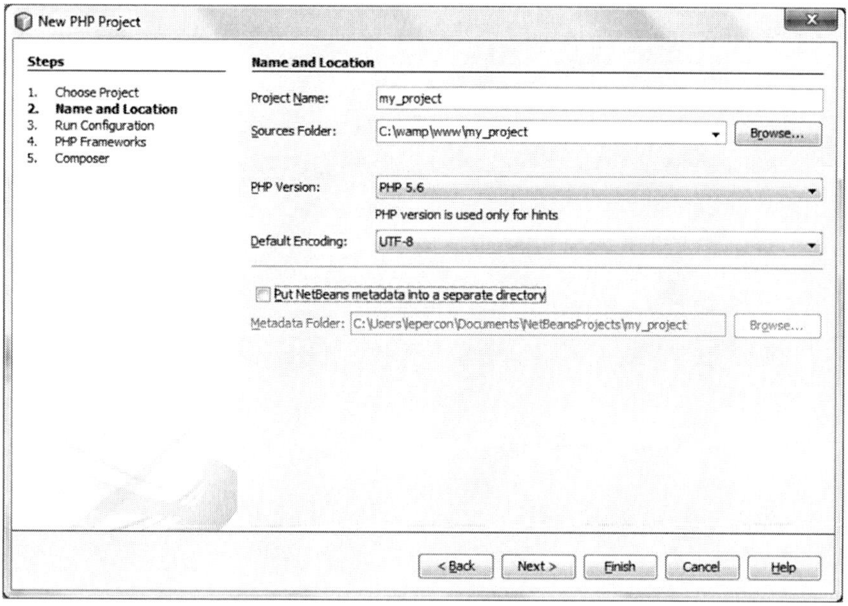

Figure 6.2. New project setup.

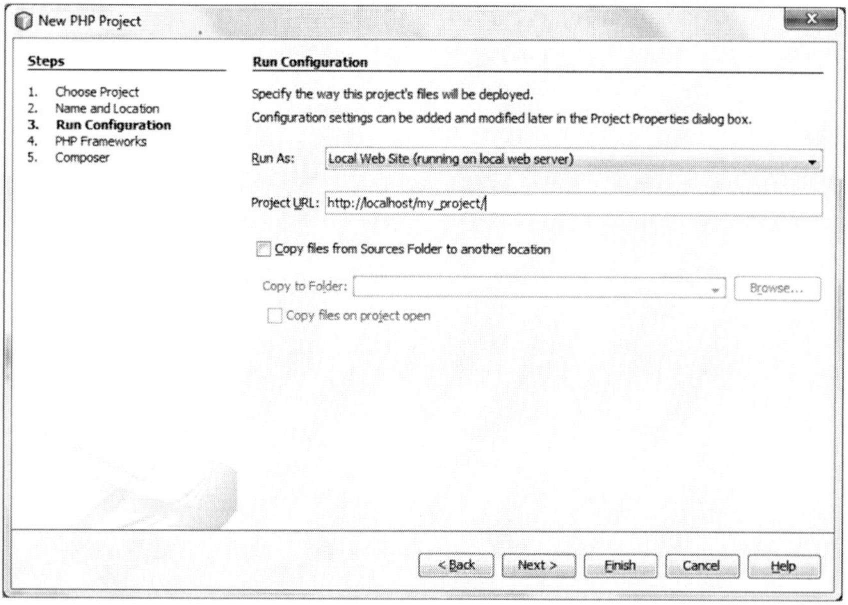

Figure 6.3. New project run configuration.

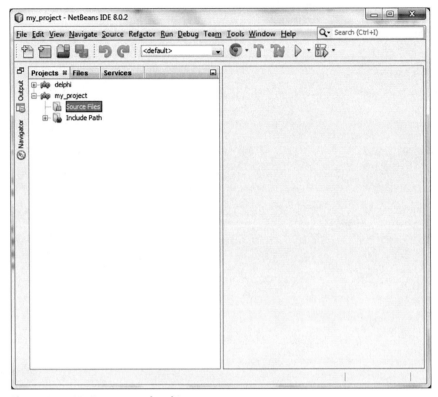

Figure 6.4. NetBeans completed setup.

The `my_project` project should now appear in the Projects Pane (figure 6.4). NetBeans is oriented into panes that can be rearranged for your screen(s) and preferences. The panes referred to in this tutorial include the Projects, Files, and Editor panes. Should any of these panes be difficult to identify, select Window followed by the name of the pane to toggle the visibility of the pane off and on.

To test that NetBeans and WampServer are working together, create a new file in `my_project` called `index.php`.

- Select File > New File.
- Select PHP File under the File Types, then Next.
- Use `index` as the file name. NetBeans will append the .php extension automatically.
- Select Finish.

If NetBeans and WampServer have been configured correctly, visiting http://localhost/my_project should yield a blank page without any errors as shown in figure 6.5.

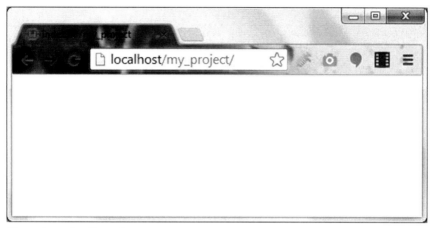

Figure 6.5. Configuration screen.

Unlike traditional programming languages, PHP can be previewed as quickly as the development environment can save the file. In other words, PHP does not require the script to be compiled before the server can accept files. The disadvantage is that all of the files related to the requested page must be pulled into memory and compiled "live" each time the script is requested. This leads to a major consideration: projects that require a significant number of memory-intensive resources may perform faster with compiled languages, such as Java. Applications that would not be ideal PHP candidates are those that index large numbers of documents. "Large" cannot be accurately specified as it depends on the actual production environment and the size of the documents; however, given a library's role as a data aggregator, this consideration is significant. Convoluting the issue further, there are caching extensions in PECL that minimize the frequency with which the server must recompile scripts.

Speaking PHP

If PHP is treated like a language, it can be approached as similar to learning a foreign language. The basic building blocks of any language are nouns and verbs. If PHP were a written language, variables would be nouns. Variables hold the information about who, what, when, where, and why. Functions, statements, and operators are the verbs of PHP, while operators can also serve the same role as adjectives. This comparison should not be held too literally; however, it can be eerily helpful. Additionally, analogous to written language, PHP syntax is equally arbitrary except that the sequence of words has been mutually negotiated between the speaker (the code) and the listener (WampServer) to avoid confusion. Examples are shown in table 6.1.

Table 6.1. Example of PHP Compared to English

English	PHP
John is ten.	`$john = 10;`
Mary is two more than John.	`$mary = 2 + $john;`
Close the door with your foot.	`close ("door", "foot");`
Say you're sorry.	`echo "You're sorry";`
What do you know about Mary?	`$raw_results = $mysql_connection->query("SELECT age, phone FROM people WHERE name_first = 'Mary'");`

Tucked into PHP syntax are some additional rules designed to add clarity for the software that will decode scripts.

- End each statement (a sentence) with a semicolon (;). This might be the most common cause of new developers' struggles because it is a tiny character that is easily missed.
- Strings should be wrapped in single (') or double (") quotes, `"like this"`.
- Any characters after two slashes (//) are ignored by the PHP parser and can be used as in-line comments: `$a_complicated_variable;  // this is a comment`.
- Comments can also be created by enclosing them between `/*` and `*/`

```
/* This style of comments
can span multiple lines and contain whatever
messages the developer sees fit */
```

Operators, functions, and statements (PHP's verbs) can perform a vast number of actions. The distinction between the three have minor impact on a PHP introduction; however, the syntax of a function usually requires something it acts *on*, which is included after the name of the function in parentheses. For example, `sort($vegetables)` would perform the `sort` function on an array of vegetables, putting them in alphabetical order. Operators are simple action verbs. There are a few operators that should be familiar to their arithmetic counterparts:

- + Add, combine, or join
- - Subtract
- * Multiply
- / Divide
- % Rhombus or remainder. `7%3` is 1 because 3 goes into 7 twice with one remainder.

- . (dot) Joins strings. `echo $x . "pesos";` would output something like `30pesos`.
- = Assignment. `$mary = 12` assigns the number 12 to the variable `$mary`.
- == Comparison operator. `3 == 1+2` returns `true`. This comparison is considered "loose" because PHP will check to see if the values evaluate to be the same, so `"3" == 3` will return `true`.
- === Strict comparison operator. `3 === 1+2` returns `true`. This comparison is considered "strict" because PHP will check to see if the values are literally the same, so `"3" === 3` will return `false` because `"3"` is a string and `3` is a number. NetBeans will warn developers if they use loose comparison instead of strict comparison because, in almost every situation, strict comparisons are more stable and work faster than loose. The preference for strict comparison over loose is also a best practice as it reduces the likelihood of some security issues. PHP's lack of strict data typing can make this operator difficult to anticipate if a developer loses track of what types of variables he or she is using.
- >, <, >=, <= Greater than, less than, greater than or equal to, less than or equal to, respectively.
- ! Not. != Not equal (loose comparison). !== Strictly not equal. For example, `$josh !== "human"` is the same as `!($josh === "human")`.

There are special situations and additional operators, including bitwise operators that are excluded here. An authoritative list and descriptions for all operators is available at http://php.net/manual/en/language.operators.php. PHP has constructions for control statements similar to C (table 6.2).

PHP5 OOP

PHP's object-oriented programming (OOP) style allows developers to take advantage of advanced programming techniques, including design patterns. Other programming languages led the technology world into object-oriented programming, leaving PHP a little late to the table. As its name implies, object-oriented programming focuses on objects as a variable. An object can execute PHP code and store other variables.

There is no shortage of metaphors to help with understanding objects in a programming context. If objects are not immediately obvious, do not be dissuaded because they are, by definition, abstract. Objects are based on portions of code that allow for easy reuse. Mr. Fish, a fish, for our metaphor, is part of a school of fish where all the members of the school are identical except for age and physical position in the sea. Each fish, from its DNA, knows how to swim, eat, and blow bubbles. If we could visibly see each fish, we could determine if it

Table 6.2. Common PHP Control Statements

if	The classic programming "switch." It is usually formed with the comparison of two variables.	```if($mary > $frank) { echo "Mary is old"; }```
else	Used after an *if* statement to provide the developer a way to define code that should be executed when the if statement is false.	```if($mary > $frank) { echo "Mary is old"; } else { echo "Frank is as old or older"; }```
while	A basic loop that occurs over and over until a certain condition is false.	```$x = 0; while($x < 5) { echo $x . ", "; $x = $x + 1; }``` This would output 0, 1, 2, 3, 4,
for	A shortcut for writing *while* loops that are designed to run $x number of times.	```for($x =0; $x < 5; $x = $x + 1) { echo $x . ", "; }``` This would output 0, 1, 2, 3, 4, . Identical to the previous example with two fewer lines.
for each	A shortcut for writing *for* loops that are designed to run on each of the elements inside an array or object.	```$fruits = array("A", "B", "C"); foreach($fruits as $item) { echo $item " "; }``` This would output A B C

was swimming, eating, or blowing bubbles. If we change how Mr. Fish swims, all the fish in the school would change to swim using these new DNA changes. With a few word substitutions to this metaphor, we could be describing objects in PHP. Fish are objects, DNA is code, and schools are classes (table 6.3).

Table 6.3. English to PHP Syntax

English	PHP
Mr. Fish is part of a school of mackerel. He is four years old and ten feet underwater.	```$mrFish = new Mackerel(4); $mrFish->position = -10;```
Mr. Fish swims to the surface.	```$mrFish->swim(0);```
If Mr. Fish is blowing bubbles, he should eat.	```if($mrFish->is_blowing_bubbles) { $mrFish->eat(); }```

Developers term *properties* and *methods* as the descriptions of an object and the actions an object can perform, respectively. Position and age are the properties of Mr. Fish. Swim, eat, and blow bubbles are the methods of Mr. Fish.

Study-room reservation systems are good examples of object-oriented programming in use at libraries. Rooms need methods defined that can reserve the room, see when the room is available, and give directions to the room. Each room needs the properties that define the name, location, and room number. Reservations themselves can also be objects. Properties of reservations include the room, date, time, and patron; methods include create, cancel, approve, move room, change time, and so on. In total, a reservation system can include classes for reservations, rooms, patrons, and buildings.

Object-oriented programming with PHP also provides some much needed code and file organization. It is a best practice to create a new PHP file for each class in an application. For a room reservation system, each class would be a separate file named after the class it contains. The reservation system would be structured into files similar to the following:

- `index.php`
- [folder] `shared`

  ○ `shared.configuration.php`
  ○ `shared.database.php`

- [folder] `reservations`

  ○ `reservations.buildings.php`
  ○ `reservations.patrons.php`
  ○ `reservations.reservations.php`
  ○ `reservations.rooms.php`

Following this practice makes it more obvious to subsequent developers where to look for specific code. This organization also suggests where a developer would add a file to develop a new class. For example, a new permissions class would be in a file named `reservations.permissions.php` in the folder `reservations`. Again, there are countless ways to create and organize a study-room reservation system; however, the critical takeaway for libraries is long-term support and development. Using community standards and best practices for file management can ensure that a homegrown library project runs smoothly into the future because future developers will likely come from the developer community.

Maintaining Complex Programs in a Library with Design Patterns

Design patterns are well documented and required learning for most developers in any object-oriented language. These patterns solve complex program issues that are rather common in PHP. That is not to say that complex issues cannot be solved without design patterns or even without objects altogether. Libraries, in particular, need to be aware how their programs will be future proofed or, possibly, how a program can be shared with other institutions. No doubt, a talented programmer can invent ways of solving complex issues that a design pattern can solve; however, it obfuscates the code for subsequent or team programmers. Additionally, the growing popularity of design patterns in open-source projects suggests that library developers will need a stronger grasp of design patterns as more library software moves toward community development. While design patterns are outside the scope of an introduction, application design gives a fun introduction to solving common development challenges. The Wikipedia article on "Software design pattern" is a wonderful overview (https://en.wikipedia.org/wiki/Software_design_pattern).

EXAMPLE

This example will handle a form submission that will send user input to a database. This common task can be riddled with security issues. The frequency of this task in libraries (suggestion box, request forms, fine appeals, technology loan agreements, and more) usually suggests that libraries will implement either a homegrown form management system or Drupal forms or another open-source framework like Form Tools. This example assumes you have a local MySQL database named my_data and a table named user_messages with text fields for user_name, user_number, and user_msg.

The first file is a standard configuration file. The purpose of this file is to be a centralized file for permissions. A best practice is to change database and server passwords whenever employee changeover occurs or when the passwords may be compromised. Either of those events can occur somewhat often. Tracking down those credentials can be laborious if they are repeated in each file. Additionally, sharing a project outside your library means redacting where passwords may appear. Centralizing passwords eases these burdens.

```
C:\Wamp\www\my_project\configuration.php
<?php
$db_host = "localhost";
$db_type = "mysql";
$db_user = "me";
$db_pass = "my_password";
$db_database = "my_data";
?>
```

The index file presents a form to users. Even though the file uses the .php extension, no PHP is declared within the file.

```
C:\Wamp\www\my_project\index.php
<!DOCTYPE html>
<html>
    <head>
        <meta charset="UTF-8">
        <title>A sample form</title>
    </head>
    <body>
        <form action="sumbit.php" method="POST">
            <label for="user_name">Your name</label>
            <input type="text" id="user_name" name="user_
name">
            <label for="user_number">Your number</label>
            <input type="text" id="user_number"
name="user_number">
            <label for="user_message">Your message</label>
            <input type="text" id="user_msg" name="user_
msg" >
            <button type="submit">Submit</button>
        </form>
    </body>
</html>
```

This file accepts data from the submitted form, then sends the data to a database to be stored.

```
C:\Wamp\www\my_project\submit.php
<!DOCTYPE html>
<html>
    <head>
    <meta charset="UTF-8">
    <title>Submission page</title>
    </head>
    <body>
    <?php
        require_once('configuration.php');
        $connection = new PDO( $db_type .
            ":host=" . $db_host .
            ";dbname=" . $db_database,
            $db_user,
            $db_pass
        );

        /*
```

Traditionally, input is accessed with $_POST['var_name'] but fil
ter_input allows more sanitation options to minimize injection attack

access. `user_name`, `user_number`, `user_msg` are the values of the previous page's input name.

```
*/
$str_user_name = filter_input(INPUT_POST, 'user_name');
$str_user_number = filter_input(INPUT_POST, 'user_number');
$str_user_msg = filter_input(INPUT_POST, 'user_msg');

//this will test if the browser sent data
if($string_user_name !== null) {
    //the quote method sterilizes strings for database input
      $connection->exec("
            INSERT INTO user_messages SET
            user_name=".$connection->quote($str_user_name).",
            user_number=".$connection->quote($str_user_
number).",
            user_msg = ".$connection->quote($string_user_msg)."
      ");
echo "Thank you for your message";
} else {
    echo "There was an error.";
}
?>
</body>
</html>
```

The above example is a common demonstration of how PHP can operate. In reality, a form submission page would include CSS, images, and additional HTML for the library's branding. If this example evolved into a more complete site with nonscript material, the number of lines of PHP versus the number of lines of non-PHP could minimize its apparent impact. Discussions about modern web standards focus more on the user experience than the development required to program that experience. Given the ease of writing and reading PHP, the importance of PHP can be deceptive. Look to conferences and communities built around PHP, Drupal, Joomla, and MediaWiki to find groups that disagree. With PHP's easy and seamless inclusion in websites, it may be PHP's own fault that it can be overlooked as an important language.

SUMMARY

PHP is a widely used open-source scripting language. Frequently employed for generating dynamic page content, PHP is compatible with most servers and platforms. Overall, PHP is easy to learn, has lots of support available, and can be used for many tasks.

BIBLIOGRAPHY

php.net. 2015a. "PHP Manual." http://php.net/manual/en/index.php.
———. 2015b. "Vendor Specific Database Extensions." http://php.net/manual/en/refs.database.vendors.php.

RECOMMENDED RESOURCES

Drupal: Drupal is a powerful open-source PHP content management system capable of managing simple blogs to an entire university's web presence. https://www.drupal.org/.

Laravel Framework: Laravel is a robust framework capable of fast delivery of institution-scale web applications. This is not an introductory framework; however, it provides prebuilt solutions to tough application scenarios. https://laravel.com/.

PHP Extension Community Library: https://pecl.php.net/.

PHP-FIG: A voluntary set of best practices that focus on interoperability of PHP applications. http://www.php-fig.org/.

php.net: php.net is the authority on PHP and hosts fully searchable and free documentation. http://www.php.net.

WordPress: WordPress is a comfortable and open-source content management system originally built around blogs but has grown to support a variety of other site structures. https://wordpress.org/.

Chapter Seven

SQL

Emily R. Mitchell and Lauren Magnuson

HISTORY AND DEVELOPMENT

Structured Query Language (SQL) is a fundamental programming language for interacting with stored application data, which is the persistent data that hangs around even when you close a program or reboot your computer. It is primarily a *declarative* language, distinguishing it from *procedural* programming languages used for writing applications, such as PHP or Ruby. SQL's basic syntax is designed to create, query, update, and delete data stored in a database. SQL is used in a variety of library contexts, and understanding how it works can enable librarians to better understand the way library data is stored, retrieved, analyzed, and potentially extended to new applications and services. To understand why SQL is so important, you need to understand what life was like before SQL. Before SQL, if you wanted a program to use persistent data, you would have to tell the program exactly how to get to that information.

If you can imagine working in a library with no call numbers and trying to give step-by-step directions to a very timid and literal-minded library patron who needs to find a book, you're on the right track here. You're going to have to tell the library patron to turn around, go up two flights of stairs, turn right, go through the door, walk to the third bookshelf on the right, and select the fourth book on the second shelf from the top. If the library purchases more books that go before the book in question on the shelf, you're going to have to know about it and change your directions so that the next time someone asks for this book, you can send that person to the sixth book on the shelf instead of the fourth. If the library ever remodels, you'll have to rememorize everything from scratch.

The above is an example of what it was like dealing with persistent data in the days before SQL. The computer programmer had to know exactly where the information she was looking for was stored. If that information was moved or reorganized, the programmer's old code would fail to work and would have to be rewritten. To make matters worse, creating and managing a database in the first place took a whole other set of equally complicated skills. Clearly, the world was ready for an improved means of managing persistent data.

In 1970, E. F. Codd published a paper with a first line that read, "Future users of large data banks must be protected from having to know how the data is organized in the machine (the internal representation)" (Codd 1970, 377). In other words, you shouldn't have to memorize the exact location of every book in your library before you're able to direct patrons to them. Codd's paper was called "A Relational Model of Data for Large Shared Data Banks," and it laid the foundation for SQL: a new way of thinking about how pieces of data *relate* to each other. This emphasis on the relationships between pieces of data is why Codd called it a "relational model."

Codd's paper was very theoretical and didn't actually come up with a programming language that could do the things he was describing. He had groundbreaking ideas, but many people doubted those ideas could ever work, much less work efficiently (Anthes 2010). It would be some years before Codd's employer, IBM, reorganized its database research teams and set them to work on System R, a new database system based on Codd's ideas (Biancuzzi and Warden 2009). It would be a few more years after that before Patricia Selinger published a paper showing how systems using Codd's relational model could be made efficient enough to stand against their competition (Anthes 2010).

System R was a project that would change databases forever. Selinger was one member of the System R team, with two others being Donald Chamberlin and Ray Boyce. Chamberlin and Boyce were assigned to develop the query language to bring Codd's ideas to life. These two researchers had a number of goals for their new language, including that it should do the following:

- use English keywords that are easy to understand;
- allow users to create databases; control who has access to them; and let users add, subtract, and query information;
- be functional on its own, but also play well with other programming languages (Biancuzzi and Warden 2009).

Chamberlin and Boyce called their language SQL and published a paper on it, sharing their language with the world. This enabled other groups to move forward, implementing SQL at the same time IBM was. In fact, the first commercial SQL-based product to appear on the market wasn't from IBM at all—it was the product Oracle, from Relational Software Inc., which later went on to become Oracle Corporation. Oracle version two, the first version released to the public, came out in 1979 (Preger 2012). Oracle is still a major player in the database world today.

Since so many groups were creating their own systems based on SQL, SQL became an international standard for creating and managing relational databases in 1986. These standards have been updated and improved on through the years, adding features and solving problems (Preger 2012). However, compliance with the standard beyond a basic level has been an ongoing problem since every group implementing SQL has done so differently (Sheldon and Moes 2005).

As a result, there are many different dialects of SQL available to database developers today. Two of the most common types of SQL used in the library world are MySQL and PostgreSQL. As with dialects of a spoken, human language, these dialects are similar enough that a developer can understand most of what is said in an unfamiliar dialect without hardship. However, true fluency in a given dialect takes some effort. What this means is that all SQL databases will store information in tables, with each row in a table representing a separate entry, but the exact wording used to add information to the table, or select information out of the table, and other processes, will be different from dialect to dialect. Examples in this chapter will be given for MySQL.

It is also worth noting that there have been further advances in the world of database systems in recent years. Various types of NoSQL, or Not Only SQL, have been gaining momentum for scaling up to deal with large data sets (Vaish 2013). Some big names in the NoSQL world currently are MongoDB, CouchDB, and Hadoop, among many others.

This is not to say that SQL databases aren't worth investing the time to learn. Libraries have a lot invested in SQL databases. Most of our systems run on them, and anyone who wants to do any programming in the library world is very likely to encounter some flavor of SQL sooner rather than later.

ENVIRONMENT AND SETUP

The SQL language is a standard that is widely implemented across various relational database management systems, or RDBMSs. In order to use SQL, you'll need access to an RDBMS. For those who want to experiment with using SQL queries without necessarily installing a local RDBMS environment on a server or other computer, the University of Washington has developed an innovative project called SQLShare that enables users to upload data and run SQL queries freely through the SQLShare interface. Several examples used in this chapter can be run utilizing the SQLShare platform.

If you want to really dig into learning and applying SQL, though, you'll probably want to install a local RDBMS environment. Examples of these environments include MySQL, SQLite, or PostgreSQL. All three of these are popular open-source RDBMSs that can be downloaded for free and installed on a server or other computer.

MySQL is an integral part of a common server setup (or stack) known as LAMP (Linux Apache MySQL PHP). A LAMP server utilizes a Linux operating system, an Apache web server to deliver content via a web browser, a MySQL RDBMS, and PHP to write applications. Thus, if you have access to a LAMP server, it already has MySQL installed and ready to go.

Analogous software packages that can be installed on OS X or Windows computers include MAMP (for Mac OS X), or WAMP/XAMPP (for Windows). Such stacks are often used to develop software on your own computer rather than a server. If you have installed MAMP or WAMP, you can use it to turn on a web server hosted on your own machine, which allows you to "host" web pages and web applications on your own computer (referred to as "localhost").

When you're using MySQL, it's good to keep in mind that MySQL itself is designed for command line interaction and does not have a native graphical user interface (GUI). However, tools exist to shield MySQL users from having to use the command line. For example, phpMyAdmin is a common MySQL interactive interface that is packaged with LAMP-style software stacks. phpMyAdmin can be used to create and delete ("drop") MySQL databases and tables without requiring command line interaction.

That being said, knowledge of the MySQL command line is useful when working with custom applications. Extensive documentation for interacting with the MySQL command line is available (http://dev.mysql.com/doc/refman/5.5/en/mysql.html). A sample of command line operations used with MySQL are provided in the "Examples" section of this chapter.

USES

SQL environments are present in a variety of applications utilized in libraries, including integrated library systems (ILSs) and resource sharing systems, website content management systems (CMSs), digital asset management systems (DAMSs), and more.

Integrated Library and Discovery Systems

SQL is found in multiple integrated library and discovery systems, including these:

- Koha open-source ILS (MySQL)
- Evergreen open-source ILS (PostgreSQL)
- Sierra Innovative Interfaces Inc. ILS (PostgreSQL)
- Intota ProQuest ILS (Microsoft SQL)
- VuFind open-source discovery interface (MySQL)

Within ILS and discovery applications, an understanding of SQL syntax is increasingly useful in order to customize data gathering from these systems. Knowledge of SQL syntax can enable libraries to gather and report data that may not be directly built into the software as a "canned" report.

For example, data stored within Koha's open-source ILS can be queried directly, and Koha users have gathered extensive documentation for writing custom queries (http://wiki.koha-community.org/wiki/SQL_Reports_Library). Reports typically involve pulling data out of the database or, as an SQL user would say, *selecting* that data. Queries in Koha can vary somewhat from straightforward SQL requests, but the basic syntax will quickly become familiar to you as you get to know SQL. The Koha example below retrieves a specific MARC tag (stored as MARCXML) from Koha's `biblioitems` table (http://wiki.koha-community.org/wiki/SQL_Reports_Library#Query_MARC):

```
SELECT
      ExtractValue((
          SELECT marcxml
          FROM biblioitems
          WHERE
              biblionumber=14),
              '//datafield[@tag="952"]/subfield[@
code>="a"]') AS ITEM;
```

Innovative Interfaces' Sierra ILS allows libraries to create custom applications that directly query the library's PostgreSQL database in order to create new services or reporting mechanisms. For example, see this Ruby on Rails application that supports record models in Sierra's PostgreSQL database: https://github.com/uclibs/active_sierra. Documentation for Sierra customers (authentication required) is available here: http://techdocs.iii.com/sierradna/app. With knowledge of SQL, a library could, for example, "write a script or application that pulls acquisitions transactions data out to load into

an external accounting system" (http://blog.sierra.iii.com/feature-spotlight
-sierradna-application).

Content Management and Digital Asset Management Systems

Many of the most popular content management systems utilized by libraries
(Connell 2013) utilize MySQL, including the following:

- WordPress
- Drupal (can also use PostgreSQL or SQLite)
- LibGuides
- Fedora Commons–backed digital asset management systems, including
  DSpace, Hydra, and Islandora (which also uses Drupal). These repositories
  can use a variety of RDBMSs, including MySQL, PostgreSQL, SQLite,
  Oracle, and MS SQL server. Visit https://wiki.duraspace.org/display/FE
  DORA37/Installation+and+Configuration#InstallationandConfiguration
  -PrepareDatabase.

For administrators of library CMSs, knowledge of SQL syntax and schemas
is essential for troubleshooting problems within the application, backing up
and recovering data in the CMS database, and writing additional customizations, such as Drupal modules or WordPress plug-ins that store and access additional data in the existing CMS database. For a list of library-centric Drupal
modules, see https://groups.drupal.org/libraries/modules.

Additional library applications include the following:

- Guide on the Side, a tutorial application developed at the University of Ari-
  zona, utilizes MySQL to store tutorial data, metadata, and user information
  (http://code.library.arizona.edu/gots/).
- Illiad, Odyssey, and Ares (OCLC/Atlas Systems) resource-sharing systems
  all utilize Microsoft SQL (MS SQL) server.
- SFX (ExLibris) link resolver software utilizes MySQL.

PROS AND CONS

SQL exists to deal with persistent data, but of course there are other alternatives.
For example, if all you need is a relatively short list of names and addresses, an
alphabetical list in a word-processing document (a flat file) will be enough for
you. In that case, there's no point in going through the work to set up an SQL
database. The minute you go beyond that, though, SQL comes into its own.

Imagine that your library's ILS is made up of flat files. What would this mean for basic circulation tasks? You might have a document that lists all the valid patrons, ordered by their library card numbers. When someone comes to the checkout desk and shows you her card, you open up that document and scan it until you find the corresponding entry in the document. Then you type in all the information about the book that person wants to check out, including its due date.

This might be slow, but is it really so bad? It might not seem too bad for this very basic task, but real life gets more complicated very quickly. For instance, what if you have several people working the checkout desk at once? A regular word-processing document won't be able to handle input from several workers on different computers at the same time.

Furthermore, consider what will happen when you want to know how many videos are currently overdue. You can manually go through your document and count overdue videos, but that will take far more time than anyone has to sparc. You could try to write a program that could determine this, but writing a program that could handle this query would be a complicated undertaking involving many lines of code. In addition, you probably wouldn't be able to use your document during the time your program is running—and running it will very likely take quite a bit of time.

Compare this to solving the same problem using SQL. It's true that with SQL, initial setup will be more complicated than just opening a Word document and starting to type. You'll need to begin by installing SQL and then figuring out a data schema, which is a way of consistently representing the data you want to capture. In this case, your schema should include a table of information about patrons (their names, library card numbers, and addresses). You'll also want a table of library materials that includes information such as what type of item it is, its title, its author, and so on. You'll want a third table, too, showing what is checked out, who checked it out, and when it is due. You could draw a picture of your schema that looks like figure 7.1.

The fields listed in each box will become columns in a table when you implement this in SQL. Each patron's information will be a row in the table

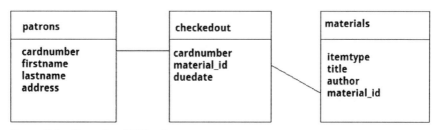

Figure 7.1.   Example of SQL schema.

of patrons; each book or video will be a row in the table of library materials; each item checked out will get a row in the table of checked out items, from which it can be removed when the item is returned.

Once you're done setting up your SQL database, though, you'll be able to work much more quickly than you would have been able to work with your word-processing file. Want to look up someone by library card number? Query the database to select the whole entry in the patron table where the `cardnumber` matches. Want to run a report telling you what videos are currently overdue? Join the materials and `checkedout` tables and select just the videos whose `duedate` has passed.

In short, flat files are

- Easy to set up and understand
- Difficult to keep current and accurate
- Nearly impossible to use for running reports

SQL is

- More complicated to set up
- Easy to keep current and accurate
- Easy to use for running reports

NoSQL databases share SQL's basic strengths. However, compared to SQL, their strengths and weakness are more subtle, in part because there are so many types of NoSQL databases. Different types of NoSQL have their own pros and cons. It's easier to say under what circumstances you might consider researching some type of NoSQL. You might be interested in NoSQL if

- you will be working with vast amounts of information (many terabytes), spread out over many different servers/computers;
- you expect to have to merge your database with someone else's database, which has been set up differently from yours.

On the other hand, you most likely will want to stick with SQL if

- you need every transaction in the database to succeed before you move on to the next transaction;
- you need to represent relationships between different types/pieces of data;
- you want as many developers as possible to be able to understand your code after you leave.

EXAMPLES

Using MySQL with a Drupal Content Management System

This example demonstrates how to create a MySQL database for use when installing a Drupal content management system. Drupal is a widely used CMS used by library websites and is also used as the front-end user interface for the Islandora digital asset management system. The commands used in this section can be used in a variety of applications requiring MySQL to create a new user, create a new database, and set user permissions.

This example presumes running a localhost server such as MAMP for Mac OS X, using Mac's built in Terminal application (found under Utilities > Terminal). The first step requires using Terminal to enter MySQL's interactive mode, which allows using MySQL's command line syntax to perform MySQL operations. To enter interactive mode, first ensure your localhost MySQL server is running (click Start Servers in the MAMP application menu). Then open Terminal and enter the following:

```
/Applications/MAMP/Library/bin/mysql --host=localhost
-uroot -proot
```

The various pieces of this command include the following:

- `/Applications/MAMP/Library/bin/mysql`—moves into the location of the MySQL software application
- `--host=localhost`—defines the host of the MySQL database as the local machine, or localhost
- `-uroot -proot`—these elements (`-u` and `-p`) refer to username and password, respectively. In this case, both the username and password are the same (root). Note that using "root" along with this kind of easily guessed username and password combination is okay for localhost development but must not be used for production applications. When using MySQL in production, it is advisable to change the root MySQL password to something hard to guess.

Terminal enters into MySQL interactive mode, which will display each line with a `mysql>` prompt, indicating that a MySQL statement is expected. While in interactive mode, MySQL commands can be entered to create users and set permissions, create and delete ("drop") databases, and more. For example, in MySQL interactive mode, the following command creates a database called `mydatabase`:

```
mysql> CREATE DATABASE mydatabase;
```

Upon entering this command, the MySQL server will report:

```
Query OK, 1 row affected (0.01 sec)
```

Whenever you enter commands in MySQL interactive mode, be sure to complete each statement with a semicolon (;) or the command line will expect additional input as part of the same entry.

Web servers utilize "ports" to serve up different access points for server applications. Applications can access MySQL data by connecting to a server's port 3306 and passing authentication credentials to perform MySQL operations. These authentication credentials are often stored within an application's configuration settings. For example, when installing a CMS such as Drupal, one step of the installation process involves entering credentials that enable the application to connect to a MySQL database (figure 7.2). Detailed instructions can be found at https://www.drupal.org/documentation/install/run-script.

In this step, the database name is the name you gave when you ran the CREATE DATABASE command (in the example above, the database name is mydatabase). Database names, usernames, and passwords are case sensitive. While you could, in development, use the same root credentials you used to access the MySQL command line, it is always advisable to create

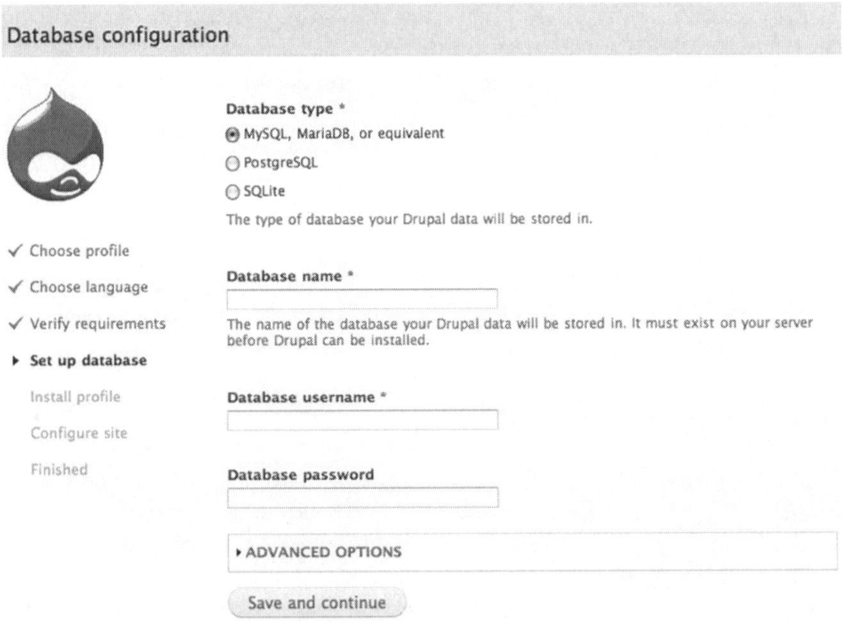

Figure 7.2.   Drupal installation: "Set up database" login screen.

unique usernames and passwords with specific permissions to the database the application needs to access. This way, if a set of database credentials is compromised or hacked, potential damage may be limited to the specific database and permissions for which the credentials were created. If credentials are limited, a hacker couldn't, for example, easily use the hacked credentials to drop or alter all of the databases in your MySQL installation. Database usernames and passwords can also be created at the command line using the following syntax, where myuser is the username and mypass is the password associated with that username:

```
mysql> CREATE USER 'myuser'@'localhost' IDENTIFIED BY
'mypass';
```

When creating database usernames and passwords for a particular database, permissions indicating what those credentials have permission to do must also be set. Permissions may vary by the application's requirements. Drupal, for example, requires a user with the following permissions:

```
mysql> GRANT SELECT, INSERT, UPDATE, DELETE, CREATE, DROP,
INDEX, ALTER, CREATE TEMPORARY TABLES ON mydatabase.* TO
'username'@'localhost' IDENTIFIED BY 'password';
```

This means that the user created for Drupal needs to be able to:

- Select data from tables in this database
- Insert new data into those tables
- Update (change) the data that is already there
- Delete data
- Create new tables
- Drop (delete) tables
- Index tables
- Change what columns are in a table
- Create temporary tables (this is useful when you get into advanced SQL)

If you need to delete a MySQL database or table for some reason, you can do it with the DROP command. For example, if you wanted to completely delete all Drupal data and reinstall the entire CMS from scratch, you would enter this command:

```
mysql> DROP DATABASE <db_name>;
```

Unless your database has been backed up, once a database is dropped it cannot be undone, so always use the DROP command with caution and be

110   Emily R. Mitchell and Lauren Magnuson

sure it is what you really want to do. A straightforward way to back up and export a MySQL database uses the `mysqldump` method as shown in the tutorial located at http://www.lampdev.org/tutorial/mysql/backup_restore/mysqldump_tutorial.html.

SQL Queries with SQLShare

This example does not require the use of an RDBMS; instead, you can utilize the University of Washington's SQLShare environment to run SQL queries and return data without installing any software locally.

To get started, download the following files from GitHub (http://github .com/lpmagnuson/sqlshare):

- `books.csv`
- `users.csv`
- `checkouts.csv`

Create an account on the University of Washington's SQLShare website, either by creating a unique account or logging in with a Google account. Upload all three files to the SQLShare website.

In the following examples, replace `youraccount` with your actual account identifier that you just created. The structure of referencing data by account name is unique to SQLShare's model and is not necessary in most RDBMS environments.

Retrieve All the English Majors

This query is fairly straightforward: which users in the user table are English majors? To just see usernames and majors, we can select those two columns from the users table using this query:

```
SELECT [youraccount].[table_users.csv].username,
[youraccount].[table_users.csv].major FROM [youraccount].
[table_users.csv]
WHERE major = 'English'
```

The output is shown in figure 7.3.

Count the Number of Users by Major

One of the most useful features of SQL is the ability to add up values and report them. The COUNT function can be used to look over a column's value and count up all the unique values. Note that the COUNT function requires a

DATASET PREVIEW   Rows **1 - 2** of **2** | Columns **2** of **2**

username	major
Parker, Amanda	English
Smith, Jane	English

Figure 7.3.   Output from **SELECT** query.

corresponding GROUP BY statement so that the SQL output knows how to display the results:

```
SELECT [youraccount].[table_users.csv].major,
count([youraccount].[table_users.csv].major) as number
    FROM [youraccount].[table_users.csv]
    GROUP BY [youraccount].[table_users.csv].major
```

Output is shown in figure 7.4.

DATASET PREVIEW   Rows **1 - 6** of **6** | Columns **2** of **2**

major	number
Computer Science	3
English	2
History	1
Math	1
Music	1
Psychology	1

Figure 7.4.   Output from **COUNT** query.

Find the Most Popular Books in This Set

In this query, we're going to use COUNT again, but this time we're counting the number of checkouts. We're going to group the output by title and order the books in a descending list so that the most popular books appear at the top of the list.

In order to display the title of the book, which is a little more readable in the output than the item number, we can use the JOIN function. This allows us to take advantage of the relationships within our data. Each book is listed in the checkouts table using a unique identifier that is also found in the book's record in the books table, letting us link the two tables together. Provided there are values that we'd expect to match in both tables, we can create a statement that finds the title from books.csv for each book listed in the checkouts.csv table. As it happens, the record_number found in books.csv is the same number set found in the item_number column in checkouts.csv so we can JOIN on that dimension:

```
SELECT [youraccount].[table_books.csv].title,
COUNT([youraccount].[table_checkouts.csv].item_number) as
checkouts
    FROM [youraccount].[table_books.csv] JOIN
[youraccount].[table_checkouts.csv]
    ON [youraccount].[table_books.csv].record_number =
[youraccount].[table_checkouts.csv].item_number
    GROUP BY [youraccount].[table_books.csv].title
    ORDER BY checkouts DESC
```

See figure 7.5 for output.

DATASET PREVIEW   Rows **1 - 4** of **4** | Columns **2** of **2**

title	checkouts
SQL for Dummies	4
The Language of SQL	4
MySQL Cookbook	3
MySQL Workbench: Data Modeling & Development	3

Figure 7.5.   Output from JOIN function.

SUMMARY

SQL is a standard that has been widely implemented across various relational database management systems. SQL comes in many different flavors, including MySQL, PostgreSQL, and SQLite. All flavors of SQL are designed to allow interaction with the persistent data stored in a database. For this reason, SQL is commonly used in conjunction with other programming languages, which typically have very different strengths. SQL's straightforward, easy-to-learn syntax has contributed to its popularity with both amateur and professional programmers in the library world.

BIBLIOGRAPHY

Anthes, G. 2010. "Happy Birthday, RDBMS!" *Communications of the ACM* 53:16–17.
Biancuzzi, F., and S. Warden. 2009. *Masterminds of Programming*. Sebastopol, CA: O'Reilly Media.
Chamberlin, D. D. 2012. "Early History of SQL." *IEEE Annals of the History of Computing* 34 (4): 78–82.
Codd, E. F. 1970. "A Relational Model of Data for Large Shared Data Banks." *Communications of the ACM* 13 (6): 377–87.
Connell, R. S. 2013. "Content Management Systems: Trends in Academic Libraries." *Information Technology & Libraries* 32 (2): 42–55.
Howe, Bill, Garret Cole, Emad Souroush, Paraschos Koutris, Alicia Key, Nodira Khoussainova, and Leilani Battle. 2011. "Database-as-a-Service for Long-Tail Science." In *Proceedings of the 23rd International Conference on Scientific and Statistical Database Management (SSDBM '11)*, ed. Judith Bayard Cushing, James French, and Shawn Bowers, 480–89. Berlin: Springer-Verlag.
Preger, R. 2012. "The Oracle Story, Part 1: 1977–1986." *IEEE Annals of the History of Computing* 34 (4): 51–57.
Sheldon, Robert, and Geoff Moes. 2005. *Beginning MySQL*. Hoboken, NJ: John Wiley & Sons.
Vaish, Gaurav. 2013. *Getting Started with NoSQL*. Olton, UK: Packt.

RECOMMENDED RESOURCES

Kriegel, Alex. 2011. *Discovering SQL: A Hands-On Guide for Beginners*. Indianapolis, IN: Wiley.
MySQL 5.6 Reference Manual. http://dev.mysql.com/doc/refman/5.6/en/index.html.
Oppel, Andrew, and Robert Sheldon. 2009. *SQL: A Beginner's Guide*. New York: McGraw-Hill.

Shaw, Zed A. 2010. *Learn SQL the Hard Way.* http://sql.learncodethehardway.org/book/.

Silberschatz, A., H. Korth, and S. Sudarshan. 2010. *Database System Concepts.* Boston: McGraw-Hill.

W3Schools PHP MySQL Database. http://www.w3schools.com/php/php_mysql_intro.asp.

Chapter Eight

C

Tim Ribaric

HISTORY AND DEVELOPMENT

C is one of the most enduring computer programming languages. Unlike other languages that were created in the 1970s, C is still actively used to develop many applications. Contrast this longevity, for example, with code written in FORTRAN. Many institutions with legacy systems have additional development costs allocated exclusively to make sure these systems continue to operate, mostly because new programmers do not spend time developing FORTRAN skills (Horton 2006). In contrast, code written in C doesn't have the same upkeep costs since programmers with an understanding of modern languages de facto have some workable knowledge of C (Bhaskar 2012).

Since C is a common ancestor of a series of newer languages, including C++, Java, Objective-C, and Python, understanding the syntax and semantics of C provides a great basis for understanding these newer languages. However, there is an interesting dichotomy floating around the industry. Some professionals have advocated that C should be the first language any programmer embarks on since it provides the right combination of syntactic structures and imparts an understanding of how memory is allocated and used (Bhaskar 2012). On the other hand, some have argued that writing good code in C is very difficult due to exactly the same rationale. In fact, poorly written C might end up being a liability as it sometimes exposes every obscure security problem. The recommended resources at the end of this chapter include a sampling of this discussion.

As an information professional, you'll probably never have a direct reason for developing an application or web service in C; however, having an understanding of it will inform everything else you'll do with programming as every language out there can classify itself as C-like or not C-like. That might seem like a tautology, but the resonating characteristics of C do lend themselves to such comparisons. Think of C as Latin since modern programming and paradigms are built on the root words of C. Unlike Latin, however, C is not a dead language. In fact, it is thriving now as much as it ever has in its four-decade history.

C was the result of the work of Ken Thompson and Dennis Ritchie, who were employed at AT&T Bell Labs (Stackhouse 1996). During the years 1969–1973, Thompson and Ritchie were working on a language to reimplement the UNIX operating system, and this work first began using a language called B. The result was a great success as it allowed UNIX to be written in hardware-agnostic language C (Bhatt 2012). For example, a development team just needed to write a C compiler in Assembler and then compile the C code using that compiler. Up until this point, an operating system was written in the lowest-level language, called Assembler (Horton 2006). This means that the operating system was tied very heavily to the Assembler used to write it. So, for example, if a new chip came out with more memory on it, the Assembler would have to be rewritten to accommodate the new chip, meaning essentially a rewrite of the operating system. In the new development paradigm, after a new chip is invented, you simply need to write a new C compiler in your Assembler to build UNIX for that hardware (Rajaraman 2012). This is considerably easier than rewriting the whole operating system.

As years progressed, however, C began to undertake different authoritative versions as computer hardware and understanding evolved. The underlying mechanisms, however, were consistent through these iterations, so knowing one type was sufficient to know about them all. The major epochs were the following:

- K & R—Named after the authors of the original language specification, Kernighan and Ritchie, first seen in the early 1970s.
- ANSI C—Came into existence officially in 1989 and was the first attempt to create a more complete, standardized version of C so that it could begin to be used with the new fledging microcomputer home market. Up until this point, C was mostly for mainframe use.
- C99—First finalized in 1999, its goal was to introduce a new collection of features that allowed for such things as in-line functions and variable-length arrays.
- C11—Work on this version first began in 2007, but the first official specification was published in 2011. Much like the C99 iteration, this version of C sought to add more features to the language.

It is fascinating to note that after more than forty years, C is still being actively expanded and improved. This is a testament to the ubiquity and usefulness of the language. What then about the descendants of C? Knowing that C is a general-purpose language useful for implementing UNIX, what were its progeny, and when did they first begin? A comprehensive look would take volumes, but here are some of the highlights:

- C++—An extension of C that introduced a programming paradigm called object-oriented programming; the specification of this was first released in 1983.
- C#—Pronounced as if it were a music note: *C-sharp*. It can be seen as a progression of both C and C++, developed by Microsoft to be utilized on its proprietary .NET platform. It was first released in 2000.
- Objective-C—A slight extension of the C language heavily used by Apple for the OS X and iOS operating systems, also first seen in 1983.
- Python—Quite often Python is the language of choice for those interested in learning to program, especially in the past few years. It is a language built on top of C whose primary aim is to create code that is human readable and can encapsulate very complex operations in short snippets of code. Python was first introduced in 1991. Having a good understanding of C allows a coder to really appreciate the beauty and complexity that Python programs are capable of.

USES

As mentioned above, the initial use of C was to implement the UNIX operating system. As time progressed, C demonstrated that it is very useful for writing all sorts of applications (Klemens 2014). C requires a large amount of understanding from the programmer who chooses to use it. The language doesn't provide a completely structured environment where all modules/libraries are interactively included when needed. However, not all C use is esoteric or operating system specific. One interesting field where knowledge of C is handy is with the Arduino microcontroller (Purdum 2006). The Arduino is a miniature, credit-card-sized board that has been one of the key components of the recent makerspace trend.

Figure 8.1 shows a modern Arduino board known as Yun. Its defining feature is that it has built-in Wi-Fi. The paper clip is to demonstrate scale. An Arduino is a device that lets you make hardware devices that interface with your computer through a variety of different components attached to the board (Purdum 2006). Think switches, buttons, LCD displays, and infrared emitters as possible components. These sensors are plugged into the series of black plugs. The code you write for the Arduino is more or less a flavor of C.

Figure 8.1.   Yun, an Arduino board.

PROS AND CONS

A programming language can't really enjoy a forty-year lineage without have some endearing qualities. On the downside, these good qualities are pretty specific.

Pros

Fast and Utilizes Hardware Well

The primary and obvious benefit to using C is that it utilizes the computer/machine it is working on very well. Thus, you can find C programs running on embedded systems that are running UNIX or some variation of it, such as Linux. The Internet router in your home is most likely running a version of Linux on a low-powered processor. Sending out radio waves through the Wi-Fi antennas is probably made possible by some sort of C code. OpenWrt, a popular after-market operating system for home routers, is a version of UNIX that ships with utilities written in C (Kernighan and Ritchie 1978). OpenWrt is the operating system powering the LibraryBox, which is a stand-alone Wi-Fi-powered file-sharing outpost.

Extensive Support and Existing Products

Since C has been around for so long, chances are there is a library already written that your program can us. For example, if you are writing some software that uses cryptography, you can utilize a library called `cryptlib`, which is written in C and can perform all of the complicated math you will ever need. In fact, many open-source applications are compiled C products. For example, OpenSSL, a software package used to secure the HTTPS traffic in your web browser, is a C program.

C Is Ubiquitous

Although you may code and create programs in other languages, the underlying compiler that the language uses might in fact be written in C. As mentioned earlier, the Python programming language is itself an offshoot of C. With a little bit of work, it is possible to compile a Python program to a corresponding C program, which quite often is done so the code runs quicker. Consider also the extremely popular and ubiquitous web language PHP. The underlying software used to interpret the language is a platform called Zend Engine, which is written in C.

Cons

Integration into a Web Environment

Most budding coders today are interested in creating web-based services. Thus, the most popular form of development these days seems to be making apps that are accessed via a web browser. Unfortunately, C does not lend itself well to this. If pressed, you could utilize a Common Gateway Interface (CGI) program where a web server could render a web page and include the output of a C program in the final HTML (Oliphant 1997). While C is a possibility with CGI programming, Perl is often the language of choice for this kind of setup. Couple this with the idea that CGI web programming, in general, is never really a first choice for web developers (Dowling 2005). There are other, more reliable ways to generate dynamic web content; unfortunately, C isn't well suited for this.

GUI-Based Applications

Since C was born on the UNIX command line, it is mostly capable of creating programs for the command line. If you'd like to create a desktop application to run in a GUI, you'll need to spend some time learning how to use an external library that renders Windows in the interface. This could be something along the lines of GTK+. Contrast this, for example, with Visual Basic, which allows you to interactively draw widgets and forms and add code in a fluid, interactive process.

ENVIRONMENT AND SETUP

Putting an environment together to write and compile C programs is a bit different for each operating system. In a Linux or Mac OS environment, the basic tools come right out of the box, while in a Windows environment, some additional tools need to be installed on the computer. This difference originates in the lineage of these two categories of operating systems. UNIX and its descendants are something called POSIX compliant. The acronym stands for Portable Operating System Interface, which is a standard written by the IEEE that outlines some must-haves for an operating system. Most of these prerequisites have to do with C implementation details and other specific Linux utilities. The way Windows evolved was separate and distinct from UNIX, so POSIX compliance was never a driving factor with that operating system. The important thing to remember is that the main goal of the POSIX standard was to ensure compatibility between systems (Isaak 1990). This goes hand in hand with the previously stated original objective of C to be a language that can be used to build UNIX through a compilation of C code. POSIX-compliant operating systems implicitly ship with all the tools you need to write C code. Windows, on the other hand, is not a POSIX-compliant operating system, and getting the basic tools together requires the installation of a piece of software that makes your Windows computer behave more like a UNIX-based machine (Daintith and Wright 2008). However, you wouldn't want to start writing enterprise-level code after setting up your computer using the methods described below; this chapter is strictly a crash course that will provide you with just a taste of what C is and how it differs from other languages.

Linux and Mac OS

As just mentioned, the tools are available out of the box. Our investigation will use two tools. Firstly, GCC, which stands for GNU C Compiler. If you open a Terminal window and type `gcc` and hit enter, you'll probably see some error and a message such as `compilation terminated`, which actually means that it was completed. Great, that was easy. Secondly, use any text editor to enter code. We'll use nano. In both Linux (in this case Ubuntu) and Mac OS, nano comes preinstalled. To verify, open a Terminal and type in `nano`. You'll see a rudimentary interface drawn to the screen. Hit Ctrl + X to exit. Done. Compare this now with the instructions for Windows.

Windows

A version of the C tools you'll need doesn't ship with Windows. If, however, you have some version of Microsoft's Visual Studio installed, it will come with the needed tools. In our case, though, we are going to do something different. We are going to install a utility called Cygwin. Cygwin is essentially a piece of software that will help you to recreate a Linux environment in Windows. The added benefit of Cygwin is that it allows you to run other interesting and very helpful UNIX shell commands, such as `more` and `echo`. More on these later. Traditionally speaking, learning C goes hand in hand with UNIX; you would be best served to spend some time getting comfortable on a command line to get the full flavor of the experience.

To begin, download the correct version of Cygwin from http://cygwin .com/install.html. To make things easier, try the 64-bit release first and then try the 32-bit if that doesn't work. Once you run the file you downloaded, you'll be prompted with a lot of click-throughs. You'll need to pick a download site (figure 8.2); any site will do.

You can also pick a site that is geographically close to help speed up the download. Just look for domain names that match your locale. Once the base system is installed, you'll be prompted to install the packages you want. There are many options available here, but all we want to do is expand the

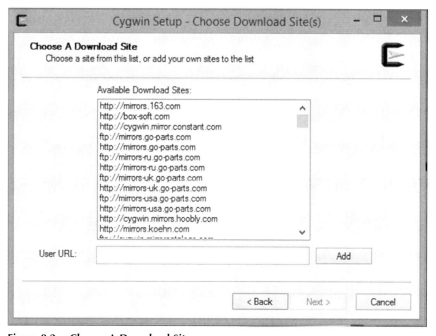

Figure 8.2.   Choose A Download Site screen.

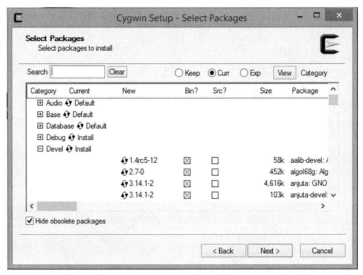

Figure 8.3.   Cygwin setup Devel install.

Devel box and click on the double arrow so that everything will be installed. It should look like the image in figure 8.3.

The box under "Bin?" changes from an empty square to a checked square. Now search for "nano," expand Editors, click on Skip to toggle it to a checked square (figure 8.4).

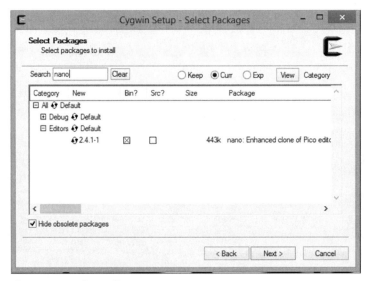

Figure 8.4.   Select Editors screen.

Hit Next a couple of times, wait for the download, and install. Click Finish at the last step to complete the process. Look for Cygwin Terminal or something similar in your start menu. The result is a box with a blinking cursor ready for you to type away.

EXAMPLES

Before we can begin with some actual examples, we need a general overview of the steps involved in creating a C program:

- Write the source code of the application. Source code has the extension c.
- Compile the source code into an intermediate "object file" that is something halfway between human-readable code and the binary instructions that the computer will run.
- Link the newly generated object file with additional object files that introduce the necessary built-in library functions required by the application. For example, if your program includes code that manipulates files, you'll need to link to object files that provide this functionality. The human-readable versions of these built-in functions are kept in header files that have the extension h.
- The final step is to create an executable file that can be run stand-alone on the Terminal command line.

In our examination, we'll be abbreviating some of these steps to make things a bit easier to follow.

Hello World

Open a Terminal window (or Cygwin, depending on your operating system) and type the following:

```
nano helloworld.c
```

You'll be greeted with a rudimentary text-editor interface. Type in the following exactly as it is written:

```
/* Hello World program */
#include<stdio.h>
main()
{
    printf("Hello World\n");
}
```

Hit Control + O to save the file. Then Control + X to exit. Once you have returned to the command line, type the following:

```
gcc helloworld.c
```

This will compile and link your program into an executable file.

```
ls
```

This will show you the contents of the current folder/directory.

```
./a.out
```

This will run your program. `a.out` is the default program name that `gcc` compiles to.

We prepend `./` to the beginning of the command because we are saying look in the present directory first. The `.` is a shortcut operator that references the current directory. When we want to refer to something that is in a directory, we use the `/` character.

After all of this wizardry, only the most basic of tasks has been completed. This is the output from the command terminal after following all of the steps:

```
>nano helloworld.c
>gcc helloworld.c
>ls
a.out helloworld.c
>./a.out
Hello World
>
```

Before looking at the actual code line by line, it is worth pointing out the tight coupling between Linux and C. Now to the code listing. Let's go line by line.

Line 1 is a comment line. Anything written between `/*` and `*/` is there for the sake of the human reading the code. The C compiler just skips that line.

Line 2 is an include statement that essentially tells C to include the libraries for standard input and output. Every program you write that does anything interesting will require this line. It is a header file that lets you use functions like `pritntf` that we will see later. Put simply, a header file is a human-readable version of the object code of those input/output functions.

Line 3 starts the main function of the program. It is preceded with a keyword void. Void is a reserved word in C and indicates that the function won't provide any returning value. We'll see an example later where we want that main function to return an integer. Anytime you write and compile a C program, it will look for the main function and run whatever it finds there first.

Line 4 is the opening brace of the main function. Anytime you define a function in C, you need opening and closing brace characters. The great thing is that C doesn't care about indentation or white space. These only exist for the sake of the humans reading the code.

Line 5 is the payload of this program. This `printf` statement is a function that takes the supplied argument, in our case the quintessential introductory statement every programmer begrudgingly learns, and prints it to standard output. In most cases, the output will be the screen. The bit about \n at the end of the string is an escaped character that appends a new line to the end of the string. After `printf` is a semicolon. Every line of code in C needs to be terminated with a semicolon, with the exception of the include line. With this obligatory example out of the way, let's delve into something particularly C-like.

Addresses of Values

Back at the command prompt, try using nano to start a file called `address.c` and then enter the following text and save the document:

```
/* Looking at the address of a variable */
#include <stdio.h>
main() {
int x;
int y;
x = 3;
y = 7;
printf("Value of x is: %d and located: %p\n",x,&x);
printf("Value of y is: %d and located: %p\n",y,&y);
}
```

The command line workflow for this example should look like this:

```
>nano address.c
>gcc address.c
>ls
address.c a.out a.helloworld.c
>./a.out
Value of x is: 3 and located: 0x7ffe28fd9a08
Value of y is: 7 and located: 0x7ffe28fd9a0c
>
```

Your output will be different than what is in the image, and we will go line by line, skipping the parts we saw with the first bit of code. Lines 4 and 5 declare two integers. A fundamental data type of any language, values are assigned to the newly created integers in lines 6 and 7.

Lines 8 and 9 are where we see C in action. We once again use `printf` to print some values to the screen. `printf` is a pretty versatile function that does more than you can imagine. If you provide it a string of text with a % character embedded in it, it will take other variables provided as arguments into the spot where the % is located. In our first example, we print x using the %d sequence. Another C-ism in action: C doesn't really know what is in any memory address, so by doing %d you are telling the interpreter to print the contents of that memory address as if it were an integer. You would use %s if you had a string you wanted to put in the sequence, %f for float, and so on. The second part is a %p, which stands for pointer. The third argument of `printf` is &x, which is the address in memory where x resides. The & operator tells C you want the address of the thing you are looking at, not the value of the thing.

The purpose of this example is to show you just how low in level you can get with C code. When we print the two integers, we first print their value. Then we do something really obscure: we print the address of the bit of memory where that value is stored (for x this is 0x7ffe28fd9a08). This ability to look at the address where something is located is a fundamental piece of C, and this mechanism is called a pointer. Understanding pointers is a lifelong pursuit, and anyone who claims to have a great understanding of them probably doesn't. Since C doesn't have object-oriented features, or highly abstracted data structures like other languages such as Python, when you want to do something complex you usually pass a pointer to the start of your complex thing. For example, an array of *n* integers is actually just *n* sequential spots in memory that are the size of integers long. When you want to reference the third item in the array, you basically reference the contents of the memory located at an offset of plus two from the memory address of the first item in the array. Recall what was said earlier about bad C creating problems. If you are accessing the contents of memory directly, it might very well be possible that you write or read a value you weren't supposed to.

Before moving to the next example, it is worth looking at the difference between the two memory addresses of the integer variables. These numbers are written in a notation called hexadecimal. So you count from 0 to 9 and then A through F before adding a placeholder. For example, when you are counting in decimal (our usual method), when we go from 9 to 10 we start a new column (the 1) followed by the 0. In hex, you start the new column after F. Just to keep things from getting even more confusing, we use a prefix 0x every time we write a hexadecimal number. In our code, we have two integers that most likely have been placed in consecutive spots in the computer's memory. The difference between these two addresses is 0x4. Therefore, an integer takes four bytes of memory. Yup, C is all about this kind of stuff. Great, why should we care? The next example tries to illustrate the importance.

Oops

Use nano again to edit the file `oops.c`:

```
/* Accessing a bit of memory */
#include <stdio.h>
main () {
int oops;
oops = 8;
printf("Address of oops is: %p\n",&oops);
printf("Contents of oops is: %d\n",oops);
printf("Address of oops plus is: %p\n",&oops + 0x8);
printf("Contents of oops plus is: %d\n", *(&oops + 0x8));
}
```

The output of the terminal after the program is entered and the compiler has been run should look like this:

```
>nano oops.c
>gcc oops.c
>ls
address.c a.out helloworld.c oops.c
>./a.out
Address of oops is: 0x7ffdff637dfc
Contents of oops is: 8
Address of oops plus is: 0x7ffdff637e1c
Contents of oops plus is: 32765
>
```

So, much like the previous example, we declare an integer and display its address in memory (line 6) and then its value (line 7). Next we grab a random address that is 0x8 away from `oops` and display that (line 8) and its contents (line 9) to the screen with the puzzling result of 32765. What is that value? What uses it? I'm not sure. The only thing I can say is that this location in memory is eight bytes higher than the memory address of oops. Let's extend this investigation to demonstrate an exploit using this idea of accessing memory you aren't supposed to.

Overflow

Try this bit of code and save into a file named `overflow.c`:

```c
/* Buffer Overflow */
#include <stdio.h>
#include <string.h>
int main()
{
    int super_user = 0;
    char login[10];
    printf("Enter username: ");
    gets(login);
    if (strcmp("bob",login) == 0 )
{

    super_user = 1;
}

    if(super_user)
{

    printf("Super Access granted!\n");
}

    else
{

    printf("Sorry, you are not a super user\n");
}

    /* Do some other things only a super user can do */
    return 0;
}
```

The following shows the output of the code writing-save-compile cycle with a few additional runs of the final product. Notice we have to pass some extra information to GCC by way of command line parameters to shut off some built-in protections the compiler usually uses.

```
>nano overflow.c
>gcc -wall -fno-stack-protector overflow.c
>ls
address.c a.out helloworld.c oops.c overflow.c
>./a.out
Enter username: bob
Super Access granted!
>./a.out
Enter username: peter
Sorry, you are not a super user
>./a.out
Enter username: joe
```

```
Sorry, you are not a super user
>./a.out
Enter username: abcdefghijklmno
Super Access granted!
>
```

Let's go line by line. Line 3 (ignoring blank lines) includes `string.h` so that we can use the `strcmp` call later on. In line 4, we declare that our main function returns an `int`, or integer value. This is used to make the example work as intended. Line 7 declares a character array of length 10, which is how C, for better or worse, represents strings. Line 9 lets us use the built-in `gets` function to get input from the keyword up until the user hits enter.

Line 12 compares the value entered by the user to the magical super user account name. C compares strings in a canonical way—character by character—and gives you the difference as an integer value. Thus, two identical strings have a difference of 0. In this case, if it checks out `super_user` is set to 1 or true. Line 16 denotes that if `super_user` is true, we know the user has special privileges, so we let him or her know about it using a `printf` statement. Line 22 allows us to conclude the main function without compilation error by returning an arbitrary integer 0 (line 23). Much like with the string compare, we use 0 here to mean successful, unlike the check of `super_user`, where a nonzero number means success. Yup, another C-ism in action.

This example is a contrived one to demonstrate the ability C has to create something called a buffer overflow. Buffer overflows happens when you cram too much data into a series of memory locations and something odd happens as a consequence. This simple program first asks for someone to enter a username. If that username is bob, then it grants that user super privileges. However, this program is exploitable. The author of the software thought that a username would only be ten characters long. However, if you were an enterprising individual, you could find out that if you entered in a username longer than ten characters, the program tries to cram in all of those characters into ten spots and it dribbles out into adjacent memory and causes all sorts of problems. In this case, it shortcuts the attempt to compare the entered user name to "bob" and sets `super_user` to 1 if that is the case. To beat this example even more over the head, the GCC line used to compile the program is a bit different than what we have seen so far. In this case, we are telling the compiler explicitly not to check against buffer overflows.

Mystery Code

If C looks confusing, well, that's because it is. As demonstrated previously, accessing everything in C is done at a very low machine level, down to the point of looking directly at memory locations. The data structures that you are given are pretty minimal, basically a continuous block of memory you need to very carefully reference. These low-level specifications create code that works well, but the trade-off is code that can be totally unreadable. This incongruence is taken to a shocking extreme with a series of events C coders participate in. For example, the Underhanded C Contest is a competition in which entrants have to create a piece of code that seems benign but actually performs some dubious function. In a previous year's contest, the goal was to create software to emulate an airline luggage processing system that must secretly reroute certain luggage if a particular free text note is applied to the record. The code also had to be written in a way that someone looking at it couldn't divine its purpose.

Another gem is the International Obfuscated C Code Contest. Take, for instance, this code block, which is a slight modification of some code that was submitted in 1990. Enter the following in a file called mystery.c:

```
#include<stdio.h>
v,i,j,k,l,s,a[99];
main()
{
for(scanf("%d",&s);*a-s;v=a[j*=v]-a[i],k=i<s,j+=(v=j<s&&(!k&
&!!printf(2+"\n\n%c"-(!1<<!j)," #Q"[l^v?(1^j)&1:2])&&++l||a
[i]<s&&v&&v-i+j&&v+i-j))&&!(l%=s),v||(i==j?a[i+=k]=0:++a[i])
>=s*k&&++a[--i])
    ;
}
```

Without a clear hint and some diagrams and polite description, it would most likely be impossible to infer the meaning of this code. The organizers of the contest have provided some hints on how to run this and what the results should look like. The code-entry-and-compiling step is shown here:

```
>nano mystery.c
>gcc matery.c
mystery.c:2:1: warning: data definition has no type
       or storage class [enabled default]
>echo 8 | ./a.out
```

You will probably get a bit of an error message, but it is safe to ignore. Before moving to the description and final product of this, let us look at the last line:

```
echo 8 | ./a.out
```

Here is another perfect example of how tightly coupled C is with UNIX. If we read this line left to right, `echo` is the name of the UNIX utility that echoes to the screen whatever follows it. 8 is what you expect it to be, the numeral 8. Next is the | symbol. In UNIX, this is a command line argument that essentially says take the output of the program on the left (a numeral 8 presented to the screen) and use it for the input of the next program, in our case the mysterious code we just compiled. This process is called piping. You can pipe the output of pretty much any UNIX command into any other UNIX command, which makes it possible to do very complicated operations on the computer in short order. Have a look at the output our example generates. Before reading on to see the description, can you determine what the code is doing by viewing this?

```
 #  #Q#  #
#  Q  #  #
Q#  #  #  #
#  #  #  Q
 #  Q  #  #
#  #  #Q#

 #  #  #  Q
#  Q  #  #
Q#  #  #  #
#  #  #Q#
 Q  #  #  #
#  #  Q  #
 #  #  #Q#
#  #Q#  #

 #  #  #  Q
#  #Q#  #
Q#  #  #  #
#  Q  #  #
 #  #  Q  #
#Q#  #  #
 #  #  #Q#
#  #  Q  #  >
```

In short, this code is displaying all the solutions to the "8 Queens" problem. This is where you take a chess board and try to place eight Queen pieces on the squares so that none of the Queens are attacking one another. I didn't get that either from looking at the code. In our emoticon-style diagram, a space represents a white square, a # is a dark square, and the Q is a Queen piece. The good thing about this code is that it finds the solutions for the Queens problem for whatever number you feed into it. You simply change the number from eight to something else. After you click the enter button on the last line, a large string of text will zip past the screen. This is actually a UNIX command called `more`, which will only output a screen full of text before stopping and requiring the user to hit the space bar before showing another screen full of text. Knowing what you know about the | operator, how can you modify our line from above to pipe the output from our compiled code into the `more` command? The answer to this is left as an exercise for the reader.

SUMMARY

This has been a whirlwind introduction to C that has emphasized how the language is used in a Linux-based system and demonstrated the primary uses you might implement with the language. The takeaway is that C is great at hardware programming, a situation where you want a really low-level interaction with the computer. You probably would not want to use the language for any HTML work. It isn't a plausible tool for something like that. C takes some work to understand, but the effort invested will pay dividends as you'll be able to program well since C forces you to write everything with simple data structures. You will also develop a strong understanding of the underlying operating system and where and how things are allocated in memory. These are the major tenets of C and, as time has demonstrated, are enduring qualities that keep the language relevant to this day. In other words, the more time you spend learning C, the easier every other language will be to understand.

BIBLIOGRAPHY

Bhaskar, K. 2012. "C—Past, Present, and Future—a Perspective." *Resonance: Journal of Science Education* 17 (8): 748–58.
Bhatt, Pramod. 2012. "UNIX: Genesis and Design Features." *Resonance: Journal of Science Education* 17 (8): 727–47.
Daintith, John, and Edmund Wright. 2008. *Posix.* Oxford, UK: Oxford University Press.
Dowling, Clay. 2005. "Using C for CGI Programming." *Linux Journal* 132 (April): 84–89.
Horton, Ivor. 2006. *Beginning C from Novice to Professional.* Berlin: Springer.

Isaak, James. 1990. "The History of Posix: A Study in the Standards Process." *Computer* 23 (7): 89–92.

Kernighan, Brian W., and Dennis M. Ritchie. 1978. *The C Programming Language.* Englewood Cliffs, NJ: Prentice-Hall.

Klemens, Ben. 2014. *21st Century C: C Tips from the New School.* 2nd ed. Sebastopol, CA: O'Reilly Media.

Oliphant, Zan. 1997. "Programming CGI in C." *PC Magazine* 16 (5): 235.

Purdum, Jack J. 2006. *Beginning C for Arduino.* Berlin: Springer.

Rajaraman, V. 2012. "Dennis M Ritchie." *Resonance: Journal of Science Education* 17 (8): 721–23.

Stackhouse, Jim. 1996. "The C Programming Language." http://www.csc.villanova.edu/~lab/C/.

Vine, Michael A. 2002. *C Programming for the Absolute Beginner: The Fun Way to Learn Programming.* Cincinnati: Premier Press.

RECOMMENDED RESOURCES

Websites

cryptlib: https://www.cs.auckland.ac.nz/~pgut001/cryptlib/.

Cygwin: https://www.cygwin.com/.

Evans, Jon. 2015. "Death to C." Crunch Network, May 2. http://techcrunch.com/2015/05/02/and-c-plus-plus-too/. (A look at why bad code in C is causing problems.)

GTK+ Project: http://www.gtk.org/.

LibraryBox Project: http://librarybox.us/.

OpenSSL: https://www.openssl.org/.

OpenWrt Wiki: http://wiki.openwrt.org/.

Seventh International Obfuscated C Code Contest: http://www.ioccc.org/years.html#1990.

Underhanded C Contest: http://www.underhanded-c.org/.

Zend Engine and PHP: https://www.zend.com/en/community/php.

Books and Treatises

Burch, Carl. 2011. *C for Python Programmers.* http://www.toves.org/books/cpy/. The popularity of Python has made it the first choice for many who are looking to learn how to program. This online tutorial/book is meant to introduce C to those already familiar with Python.

Klemens, Ben. 2014. *21st Century C: C Tips from the New School.* 2nd ed. Sebastopol, CA: O'Reilly Media. This is a modern treatise that talks about the role of C in today's landscape of languages. It is written for an audience that already has some understanding of programming and wishes to learn C, with a particular focus on what is still relevant.

Learn C The Hard Way. http://c.learncodethehardway.org/book/. Don't let the title fool you. This online book presents a modern course in learning C and presents over fifty tutorials demonstrating the modern uses of C and why it still matters as a language.

Miller, Evan. 2014. "You Can't Dig Upwards." http://www.evanmiller.org/you-cant -dig-upwards.html. While this thought piece isn't exactly a tutorial on the C language, it does provide food for thought on why it is an important language to spend time learning. Miller draws a parallel between producing good, secure, and efficient code and how knowledge of C provides insights on how this can be achieved.

Purdum, Jack J. 2012. *Beginning C for Arduino: Learn C Programming for the Arduino and Compatible Microcontrollers*. New York: Springer E-Books. This book introduces the Arduino microcontroller with a specific look at how the programming language used with it looks and functions like C. It is meant for an introductory audience that has not had any experience with either programming or experimenting with an Arduino.

Chapter Nine

C#

Peter Tyrrell

HISTORY AND DEVELOPMENT

C# (pronounced *See Sharp*) is a language developed by Microsoft for programming with the .NET framework. .NET is a large body of instructions, methods, and libraries that reflect all the possible tasks you could ask a computing device to do in a Windows environment. .NET is at the heart of Windows itself, and of pretty much everything Microsoft has produced in the last decade: the SQL Server database platform, MS Office, Windows phones and tablets, Windows servers and desktops, websites and web applications, and so on. It is key to understand that C# is joined at the hip to .NET and is very rarely employed in isolation without it. As a librarian, you will likely use C# to create a dynamic website, a mobile app, a command line utility, an Office plug-in, or a software application intended for Windows.

The history of C# is bound up in the story of the birth and maturation of Microsoft's .NET framework (Hasan 2012). .NET took over from earlier frameworks that had been developed separately, for various purposes, and as such were silo-like and difficult to get to work together. For example, around the time that .NET was invented in the late 1990s, the web was accelerating in importance, so naturally Microsoft released a framework to help programmers take advantage of that—it was called ASP, or Active Server Pages, and it was an early crack at a script engine for creating server-side dynamically generated web pages. That is to say, you could make web pages that changed in reaction to user input, or that talked to a database and served up the results of a query. The ASP web page had access to server knowledge and resources, unlike a static web page that was no more than the content of its HTML.

While ASP was a leap forward in what could be done with a web page, there were many limitations on its ability to interact with the Windows environment on the host server. Server-side functions were fragile because multiple applications across Windows could have a dependency on a set of functions called a COM object (or Component Object Model). A COM object might be a core Windows assembly or one created by a programmer. Only one version of a given COM object was allowed to be active at any one time, so it was all too easy for a programmer to introduce a minor change to a COM object that broke any number of applications on the same machine. This was known colloquially as "DLL hell" (a COM assembly ends in a .dll extension), and I have personally seen, as a direct result, programmers shouting very bad words very loudly.

.NET was created to solve problems of incompatibility and to do away with the heterogeneous, higgledy-piggledy nature of the programming landscape in the Windows environment. It presents a comprehensive and consistent interface to All Things Microsoft—mostly. Naturally, there are debates over the tiniest aspects of it, but on the whole, one can feel comfortable in the .NET cockpit writing Windows desktop software, an ASP.NET website, or a mobile phone app. .NET is the Swiss Army knife you must take with you into Microsoft's vast realm.

To C#, then. The reason C# was invented at all is not perfectly clear. Microsoft had a go-to language called Visual Basic, which you can still use to this day when programming .NET. The prevailing direction of .NET's evolution in the current day is toward a much more generic platform to which you can bring the language of your choice on the operating system of your choice, even Mac and Linux. But, back in the year 2000, it was deemed necessary to invent a language that would reflect .NET's philosophy and nature with a minimum of distortion, which could maximize the advantages and changes .NET brought to the table. It is also likely that corporate ego played a role, but we shall pass no judgement here on the desires of an organization to set the tone and guide the thoughts of those who would employ their tools.

C# has been compared to Java and was invented only six years after that competitor language/framework. There are superficial similarities in syntax and expression and even in their assumptions about, for example, an object-oriented approach to organizing code. An object-oriented language uses classes, or encapsulated modules of code that have some unity of function and that expose methods and properties, and these classes may be extended or inherited or interacted with by other classes. However, probably the largest influence on the genesis of C# was the C language and its derivative C++: the C# name reflects this. C and C++ were widely used by "serious" programmers, and C# was intended to act as a bridge to .NET for that audience, but

C#'s inventors also wanted to address what they saw as flaws in those earlier languages (Hasan 2012).

Although C# shares syntax features with the other C languages, it is far more managed. That is, it does a lot of work behind the scenes to ensure a "safe" environment that alleviates or negates common programming missteps. An example of this is its automated memory management and garbage collection (cleanup of unused memory). Programmers in C or C++ were required to assign memory for their code to operate in, and then make sure their code cleaned up after itself to avoid memory leaks, which could be a finicky operation. How much memory was enough to avoid out-of-memory exceptions? How much was too much, causing other components to starve? How often and how aggressively should memory be recycled after use, keeping in mind garbage collection incurs its own performance cost? Although C and C++ programmers could build the equivalent of Formula 1 race cars that purred like tigers and were highly optimized for the road ahead of them, the sheer expertise and meticulous effort required was a barrier to wider adoption of programming by the masses.

Microsoft recognized that a key to the success of its .NET framework was adoption by developers—as many developers as possible—and that the C# language must therefore strike a balance between power of expression, control over the programming environment, and ease of use. You can easily find the viral video of then Microsoft CEO Steve Ballmer at a conference around that time drenched in sweat while hoarsely chanting, "Developers! Developers! Developers! DEVELOPERS!" to a possibly surprised but quickly enthusiastic crowd (Know Your Meme 2012). Microsoft really—really—wanted to attract developers to .NET and C#, and they succeeded. Just as the burden of creation of video, photography, news, opinion, and content shifted in the late 1990s and early 2000s away from specialized experts and toward amateurs and enthusiasts, so too did programming and development find their way to a much larger body of creators who would produce the next generations of software, especially on the web. These developers have even come to wield heavy influence over the direction of .NET itself and its companion language, C#. Nowadays, C# is quite mature, and though a few dozen languages have been adapted for use with .NET, C# is still by far the most popular.

USES

C# allows you to manipulate the .NET framework, which is a representation of Microsoft's tools, services, and technologies, so the practical uses of C# are as wide ranging as the framework.

Web Applications

ASP.NET is the web development side of .NET. It is dependent on the presence of the .NET framework and employs it extensively, but it also includes other components and techniques that have nothing to do with .NET per se. These other components are all to do with producing web pages because ASP.NET may be defined as a toolbox for creating web pages that serve dynamic content. If the web page you intend to serve must make decisions when showing content, must authenticate a user, or must retrieve content from a search engine or remote API, or if it must talk to a database, or log a page's actions, and so on, then you need a programming language. This is where C# comes in.

To be clear, C# is a server-side or back-end language, which means it is executed on the server, as opposed to on the client browser as JavaScript is. The web is a stateless and disconnected environment; the browser does not have a live and continuous connection with the server. A good analogy would be the postal system: the browser mails its request to the server, which acts on the request and sends a response. In between these little bursts of activity, server and browser sit there passively, each having no idea what the other is doing, or indeed knowing whether the other side has been dragged offline by bears in the interim. C# fits into the "server acts on the request" portion of the scenario.

On the server, each response has a life cycle. For the sake of convenience, let's call the response a web page, although it could equally be raw information encoded in XML or JSON (JavaScript Object Notation), or a file, rather than an HTML document. ASP.NET provides programmatic access to events in the response life cycle, points at which you can intervene and make decisions or modify the output in some way. Practically speaking, the bulk of your code tends to reside at the same event point, that being the place where everything about the client request is available to you, along with a lot of information about the current server state.

Let's look at a typical response life cycle. First, authenticate the client request. This is the point at which users gets whisked off to the login page if they haven't logged in yet. Generally speaking, authentication is a matter of configuration in ASP.NET, and you don't need code to specifically check for authentication on every request.

Login example:

```
public class AuthenticationController : BaseController
{
    private readonly IAuthenticateService _authService;
    public AuthenticationController(IAuthenticateService
authService, ILogger logger)
```

```
    : base(logger)
    {
        _authService = authService;
    }
    [AllowAnonymous]
    public ActionResult Login(string returnUrl)
    {
        return View("Login");
    }
/*
```

Declarative attributes like [HttpPost] are metaprogramming on the method they decorate. [HttpPost] declares that this login method over-load, and not the one above, is the one that will handle POST requests (i.e., when the user has submitted the login form). [AllowAnonymous] declares that an unauthenticated user is allowed—else how could anyone login?

```
*/
    [HttpPost]
    [AllowAnonymous]
/*
```

The LoginViewModel contains the values the user entered in the login form. The returnUrl is where the user tried to get to before being redirected to the login, and where the user will be returned if the login is successful.

```
*/
    public ActionResult Login(LoginViewModel login, string
returnUrl)
    {
        if (!ModelState.IsValid)
        {
            ViewBag.Error = "Form is not valid; please
review and try again.";
            return View("Login");
        }
/*
```

Exactly how the authentication service will check the credentials is obscured here (maybe it will talk to a database), but that's kind of the point. We don't need to know at this level. That makes it easy to change how the authentication service works internally, without breaking any code dependent on it.

```
*/
```

```
    if (_authService.Authenticate(login.User, login.
    Password))
    {
/*
```

FormsAuthentication is built into .NET. The SetAuthCookie() method will add an encrypted authentication token in the form of a cookie to the response. The cookie will get passed back and forth with each request/ response from then on and will be checked each time by a built-in ASP.NET inspector so we don't have to.

```
*/
    FormsAuthentication.SetAuthCookie(login.Username,
    false);
    if (_authService.ValidateReturnUrl(returnUrl))
    {
    return Redirect(returnUrl);
    }
    else
    {
    return RedirectToAction("Index", "Home");
    }
    }
    ViewBag.Error = "Credentials invalid. Please try
    again.";
    return View("Login");
    }
    public ActionResult Logout()
    {
        Session.Clear();
        FormsAuthentication.SignOut();
        return RedirectToAction("Index", "Home");
    }
}
```

If the request is already authenticated, you still might have to check that the user is authorized to get the response. If the page is for admins only, for instance, you need to check that they belong to the admin role.

Authorization example:

```
[Authorize(Roles = "Administrator, Super User")]
public ActionResult Admin() {
    return View();
}
```

Next, examine the client request for signals on what to do. These signals might be encoded in the request URL path or parameterized in its query string as name-value pairs, or arbitrary data posted with the request package that is not dependent on the URL value at all (including cookies). There are also request headers that may be looked at—these usually contain metainformation about the request and the requestor. Then fetch any content necessary to fulfill the client request. It may be necessary to query a database or other data source.

Permalink example:

```
public class HomeController : BaseController {
    private readonly ISearchService _searchService;
    private readonly ILogger _logger;
    public HomeController(ISearchService searchService,
ILogger logger)
    : base(logger) {
        _searchService = searchService;
        _logger = logger;
    }
/*
```

The permalink URL might be http://example.andornot.com/permalink/123, but we don't actually know at this level unless we explicitly check. The URL is examined by routing code earlier, and the response is sent here with the ID portion if a permalink pattern is matched. This means you could have multiple patterns routing to this `Permalink` method.

```
*/
public ActionResult Permalink(string id) {
if (string.IsNullOrEmpty(id)) {
/*
Not giving a model to the view is the same as passing
null. The view can check to see if the model is null and
show 'no such permalink' content.
*/
    return View("Permalink");
    }
/*
```

`ISearchResults` is code we defined elsewhere to hold information about the search results returned by the search engine. The search service is also code we made to talk to the search engine. Thus "model" will encapsulate everything about the search engine query, including a result for the ID if the search was successful.

```
*/
        ISearchResults model = _searchService.Single(id);
/*
```

The View is responsible for styling and rendering the raw search result data held in the model. It's where you would see HTML.

```
*/
        return View("Permalink", model);
}
}
```

Pass raw information to the view, where it will be bound to HTML or used to make decisions on how to construct HTML.

Permalink View example:

```
@model ISearchResultModel
@{
/*
```

This view wraps itself in HTML from the common layout view.

```
*/
        Layout = "~/Views/Shared/_Layout.cshtml";
/*
```

The model contains search results as a collection of strongly typed documents. Model.Documents is of type List<Document>.

```
*/
        var doc = Model.Documents.SingleOrDefault();
        string title = doc == null ? "Bad Permalink" : doc.
Title;
/*
```

ViewBag is a dynamic collection (a "bag") built into the view. It provides a convenient way to pass arbitrary information to and between views. The title here will be assigned to the HTML title tag in the layout view.

```
*/
        ViewBag.Title = title;
}
@if (doc == null)
{
        <ul>
```

```
            <li>
                <h2>
                    <span class="text-notfound">No
document</span> found for that id.
                    <span class="divider"> </span>
                </h2>
            </li>
            <li>
                Was that a typo? Try again, or start a
                @Html.ActionLink("New Search", "Index",
"Home") instead.
            </li>
        </ul>
}
else
{
        <div class="permalink-view">
        @{
/*
```

Here we pass on the model to a shared list view, where the single search result document will be laid out in the same way it would be if it were part of a set of search results. That way we don't need to re-create the document's layout just for the permalink view, and we stay DRY (Don't Repeat Yourself).

```
*/
        Html.RenderPartial("_List", Model);
        }
        </div>
}
```

PROS AND CONS

There are two sets of C# pros and cons to consider: C# and .NET as compared to other programming frameworks, and C# as compared to other languages within the .NET framework.

C# and .NET versus Other Frameworks

The choice of which programming framework or environment to work with is fundamental: that decision will color everything you do henceforth, from the tools used to write the software to the operating systems it can be deployed to. The framework will influence your design, the way you approach problems, and even the types of problems you are likely to encounter. The framework's effects on the mind are subtle but deep, which is why frameworks tend to engender programming cultures.

The nation of Java is an ocean away from the kingdom of .NET, though both lie many miles from that continent peopled by the land of Ruby on Rails, the hegemony of PHP, and the principality of Python. These countries and a small host of others all have their distinct borders, diehard patriots, and unending rivalries. One must take any criticism of a framework by a practitioner of another with a grain of salt. And, vice versa, a recommendation may be tinged with zeal by a true believer and must be viewed with some skepticism. I suppose it is human nature to argue vociferously the merits of one's chosen group, but the truth when it comes to programming is that they are all more than adequate. You're really not going to gain a noticeable performance advantage by choosing one over the other, unless you are programming for rocketry or nuclear medicine or something similarly specialized, and in that case, you would have already picked Fortran as the obvious choice for its strengths in mathematics.

What does make sense is to choose the programming framework and language that you have ready access to, will run on operating systems you are familiar with, and that is supported and understood by people you can call on to help when help is needed. Not to mention you will probably invest years of your life in this decision—switching horses midstream is not advisable.

The following are the questions you ought to ask yourself when making a framework decision:

- Can you get the editing tools you need easily set up on your computer?
- Or better yet, can you use the editor you already have and like?
- How easy is it to debug code you have written?
- Will you be required to compile your code into an assembly or executable, or will it run as a script, as is?
- Where are you going to deploy the thing you have made, and what does the target machine require to run it? A web application needs a complex web server stack, for instance, whereas a command line utility demurely wants a few humble requirements.

C# and .NET Pros

- Well documented and widely written about, by both official and unofficial sources.
- Wide body of practitioners to commiserate and share information with.

- Mature: fifteen years of iterative releases means that C# is full featured yet filled with labor-saving shortcut expressions.
- Strong choice in a Windows environment: .NET is embedded in every Windows OS.
- Cloud server architecture is available with Microsoft Azure.
- The .NET Core Framework, ASP.NET 5 for building web applications, and the C# compiler Roslyn are open source as of November 2014 (Landwerth 2014).
- Backed by Microsoft.
- Microsoft has vast resources and a vested interest in the success and uptake of its programming framework.
- The past decade has seen Microsoft's developer arm become progressively more open and responsive to practitioners.

When using C#, there are fewer solutions and tools to choose from when approaching a problem, compared to some completely community-guided open-source frameworks. This may seem like a con at first glance, but it is a blessing in disguise. Generally, it means there is a "right" or at least "best" way to do something, often certified by Microsoft professionals, as opposed to a myriad of opinions and overlapping or even redundant tools to sift through and choose from. Democracy is a wonderful thing but not necessarily as efficient as a benevolent dictatorship.

C# and .NET Cons

- Historically tied to Windows, though upcoming releases will broaden support to MacOS, iOS, Linux, and Android.
- The complexity of the development environment, and the relative difficulty of initial setup.

Visual Studio

Your programming environment will almost inevitably rely on Visual Studio, the integrated development environment (IDE) produced by Microsoft. It is a powerful suite of tools, but its very power and complexity can be daunting. Microsoft likes to refer to Visual Studio and .NET as a developer "ecosystem," which should give you a clue as to its sheer enormity and diversity. Visual Studio is a code editor with syntax highlighting and code completion for all its included languages, plus CSS, XML, JavaScript, and other types of resources.

Code you write requires compilation into an assembly or executable, which means you need a compiler. Visual Studio is both a code editor and a compiler. It is technically possible to compile code without Visual Studio, but that is quite an advanced feat.

Debugging (that is, stepping through the source code of an assembly or executable that is currently running in order to watch what is happening as it happens) becomes necessary once your code hits a certain level of complexity. Debugging requires a debugger and some investment of time to learn how to do it effectively. Visual Studio is the only practical choice as a debugger for .NET code.

The good news about Visual Studio is that, while professional versions of Visual Studio cost hundreds of dollars per license, a free version called Visual Studio Community Edition (previously called Visual Studio Express) is available. Community Edition may be used by individual developers or those working for "non-enterprise organizations" to develop free or paid apps. The Community Edition is not function-limited like its ancestor Visual Studio Express, and the license terms are quite generous since "enterprise" is defined as an organization with over 250 PCs or greater than one million dollars in annual revenue. Even within an enterprise, Community Edition may be used to contribute to open-source projects, for academic research, or for classroom learning scenarios.

C# versus Other Languages within .NET

Over thirty languages can be used to program .NET (https://en.wikipedia.org/wiki/List_of_CLI_languages). Apart from C#, which enjoys the widest use, notable examples include Javascript, Ruby, and Python, in the forms of Managed JScript, IronRuby, and IronPython.

There are many technical features of C# that require a lot more explanation than we have room for here, and whether they are pros or cons compared to other languages depends greatly on your own perspective. Suffice it to say, C# has many tricks and labor-saving devices that will help you express your intent concisely, along with safety nets designed to save you from yourself. Here is a short list of features that will reward your efforts to learn more about them:

- Strict typing, anonymous types, type safety
- Object oriented, with multiple inheritance via interfaces
- LINQ
- Generics
- Lambda expressions and functional programming

- Nullable types
- Metaprogramming via attributes

EXAMPLES

LINQ

LINQ stands for Language-Integrated Query. It provides a set of patterns for querying and updating that smooth out and abstract away the idiosyncrasies of the data store being worked with. LINQ to Objects, LINQ to XML, and LINQ to SQL are providers included by default in the .NET framework (Microsoft Developer Network n.d.), such as LINQ to JSON and LINQ to ODATA.

The advantage of LINQ is that the patterns are relatively easy to learn and, once mastered, give you a standard approach to working with a variety of data sources. Without LINQ, you are obligated to write many lines of helper code to support the operations you are actually interested in using, and you need to understand the vagaries of the underlying data store much more deeply. Further, LINQ is able to simplify greatly statements that are complicated and messy in the original language—this is particularly true with SQL (Albahari nd). LINQ saves a lot of time and brain capacity.

Speaking of SQL, you may find LINQ operators reminiscent of SQL syntax. This is not because we are querying an SQL database necessarily but because of convergent evolution: these operators are efficient expressions. Although LINQ syntax is influenced by SQL languages, it looks the same no matter the nature of the underlying data source.

Tools Needed

You will need LINQpad (http://www.linqpad.net) or Visual Studio IDE (https://www.visualstudio.com/).

LINQ to Objects

Any object in the .NET framework that is enumerable can be manipulated with LINQ. All the built-in collection classes inherit either the `IEnumerable` or `IEnumerable<T> interface*`, and anyone can write a new collection that does the same. An interface is a template that forces you to add its named methods or properties to your own code. `IEnumerable` makes you add a method called `GetEnumerator()`, for instance. How you write that method and get it to return an `IEnumerator` object like it's supposed to is up to you. The interface just enforces the method signature.

Arrays and lists are examples of commonly used enumerable collections. We would normally use the `foreach` operator to enumerate them, but we can also use LINQ, particularly if we intend to return a subset.

```
string[] array = new string[] {"Chupacabra", "Sasquatch",
"Honest Politician"};

// load 'rarities' via foreach
var rarities = new List<string>();
foreach (string item in array) {
     if (item.StartsWith("Honest")) {
          rarities.Add(item);
     }
}

// load 'rarities' via LINQ
var rarities =
  from item in array
  where item.StartsWith("Honest")
  select item;
```

The advantages of the LINQ version might not be immediately obvious, but:

- It declares and sets the rarities variable in a single statement, which, when reading the code, eliminates any ambiguity as to what `rarities` will be used for.
- The overall purpose of the snippet is easier to understand at a glance. A `foreach` loop only tells you there is going to be an iteration, not what the iteration is going to achieve, whereas the LINQ's select operator signals the statement's intent clearly.

LINQ to XML

The XML sample has a root `Catalog` node that contains multiple `Book` nodes, where each `Book` has some basic metadata as child nodes, except `id`, which is an attribute of `Book`. Multiple authors are represented by repeated `Author` nodes.

XPath can be used to query XML, but it's awkward to implement in .NET. There is quite a difference in the following example between the functional but complicated XPath approach and the brevity of the LINQ version.

```
var rawXml = @"
   <Catalog>
     <Book id='book001'>
```

```
        <Author>Pilkey, David</Author>
        <Title>The Adventures of Captain Underpants
        </Title>
        <Genre>YA Fiction</Genre>
        <PublishDate>2013-04-30</PublishDate>
        <Description>George and Harold have created
the greatest superhero in the history of their elementary
school—and now they're going to bring him to life!
</Description>
      </Book>
      <Book id='book002'>
        <Author>Albahari, Joseph</Author>
        <Author>Albahari, Ben</Author>
        <Title>LINQ Pocket Reference</Title>
        <Genre>Nonfiction</Genre>
        <PublishDate>2008-03-07</PublishDate>
        <Description>This guide has the detail you need
to grasp Microsoft's new querying technology, and concise
explanations to help you learn it quickly.</Description>
      </Book>
    </Catalog>");
// get authors via XPath
var xml = new XmlDocument();
doc.LoadXml(rawXml);
XPathNavigator navigator = xml.CreateNavigator();
XPathExpression authorQuery =
avigator.Compile("/Catalog/Book/Author");
XPathNodeIterator iterator = navigator.Select(authorQuery);
var authors = new List<string>();
while (iterator.MoveNext()) {
    authors.Add(navigator.Value);
}
// get authors via LINQ
var xml = XElement.Parse(rawXml);
var authors =
    from e in xml.Descendants("Author")
    select e.Value;
```

The LINQ version is so much simpler! Quicker to write, easier to read. The XPATH version suffers from too many variables and a complicated multistep process. *My* eyes glaze over when I read it, and I'm the one who wrote it. The XPATH expression itself is not at fault, and indeed there are ways to work with XPATH within LINQ to XML, but in most cases you won't even need to.

SQL Example

Two tables represent Books (table 9.1) and Authors (table 9.2), with a join table in between so books can be assigned multiple authors (table 9.3). Table 9.4 shows the BooksToAuthor result.

Table 9.1.   Book Information

BookId	Title	Genre	PublishDate	Description
book001	The Adventures of Captain Underpants	YA Fiction	April 30, 2013	George and Harold have created the greatest superhero in the history of their elementary school—and now they're going to bring him to life!
book002	LINQ Pocket Reference	Nonfiction	March 7, 2008	This guide has the detail you need to grasp Microsoft's new querying technology, and concise explanations to help you learn it quickly.

Table 9.2.   Author Information

AuthorId	Name
1	Pilkey, David
2	Albahari, Ben
3	Albahari, Joseph

Table 9.3.   Books, Authors, and BooksToAuthors

Books	BooksToAuthors	Authors
BookId	Id	AuthorId
Title	BookId	Name
Genre	AuthorId	
PublishDate		
Description		

Table 9.4.   BooksToAuthors

Id	BookId	AuthorId
1	book001	1
2	book002	2
3	book002	3

SQL Query Comparison: Native SQL

Here is the select statement in Transact-SQL (T-SQL):

```
SELECT
      b.BookId,
      b.Title,
      b.Genre,
      a.Name AS Author
FROM
      Books b
INNER JOIN
      BooksToAuthors b2a ON b2a.BookId = b.BookId
INNER JOIN
      Authors a ON a.AuthorId = b2a.AuthorId
WHERE
      b.Title LIKE "LINQ%"
```

The results of the select query are shown in table 9.5.

Table 9.5. Query Results

BookId	Title	Genre	Author
book002	LINQ Pocket Reference	Nonfiction	Albahari, Ben
book002	LINQ Pocket Reference	Nonfiction	Albahari, Joseph

Even though one book satisfies the query, the result is denormalized into two rows, one for each author association. It is possible to collapse the authors into a single row with SQL, but that requires some advanced trickery. Even were the authors to be concatenated together into the same column, they would become a single string value such as `Albahari, Ben|Albahari, Joseph`. That value is readily understood by the human eye as two joined subvalues, but a computer has no idea they are separate entities unless it is told to explicitly split them apart at the separator character. This isn't an impossible task, just undesirable. The alternative is to take the two rows and write code to manually collapse them on the `id` value to accurately reflect the true nature of the data as a single title with multiple authors. Wouldn't it be better if the query results already reflected that reality?

SQL Query Comparison: LINQ

The following LINQ statement is more or less equivalent to the SQL inner join above, but explicit join syntax is not actually required to get what we need in this case. The variable `db` represents the SQL database as an object and is assumed to have been defined already when configuring LINQ as part of an object-relational mapping (ORM) process. It therefore has knowledge of the SQL tables, column types, and relationships. There, in a nutshell, is much of the power of LINQ to SQL: instead of defining joins each time we write a query, we explain those relationships up front and reap the benefits with cleaner code thereafter.

We create authors as a collection on the fly to group multiple authors together and to filter results to books that have authors.

```
var books =
     from b2a in db.BooksToAuthor
     where b2a.Books.Title.StartsWith("LINQ")
     let authors = b2a.Authors.Name
     where authors.Any()
     select new CatalogBook
     {
          Id = b2a.BookId,
          Title = b2a.Books.Title,
          Genre = b2a.Books.Genre,
          Authors = authors
     };
```

The result of the query will always be an `enumerable*` collection. In this case, the variable `books` contains a collection of `CatalogBook` objects because we create one for each item that matches the LINQ query.

We could have created an anonymous dynamic object for each item and saved ourselves the trouble of having to define the `CatalogBook` type somewhere, but the advantage of using a strongly typed class like `CatalogBook` over an anonymous object is that we will always know what to expect when dealing with it. An instance of `CatalogBook` will have an `Authors` property that is an array of values, not sometimes an array and sometimes a single value. Foreknowledge is fore . . . er, power: we can continue to use `CatalogBook` elsewhere in our code, always with the same expectations, and never have to manually interpret or convert the results of the database query.

There is another, subtler benefit to mapping database results immediately to a strongly typed object, which is that an error will occur at that point if database results do not conform to the object's expectations. An error! Well yes—and that's good. "Fail early, fail often" is advice that seems counterintuitive, but because errors can be trapped and dealt with in code, it is better to know exactly when, where, and how something has gone wrong as soon as possible. An issue allowed to slide will cause problems down the line, where it will be more difficult to diagnose and track back to its actual point of origin. "Enumerable" means that the collection can be looped through, as with the following `foreach` construction:

```
foreach (var book in books) {
    Console.WriteLine(string.Format("{0}, {1}, {2}, {3}",
        book.BookId,
        book.Title,
        book.Genre,
        string.Join("; ", book.Authors));
}
```

SUMMARY

C# is a ubiquitous server-side language that is linked hand in hand with .NET. This allows C# to work best in a Windows environment for a wide variety of tasks. Strongly supported by Microsoft, C# is well documented and widely written about. In addition to being fairly easy to learn, it also provides some safety nets to keep beginners "safe."

BIBLIOGRAPHY

Albahari, Joseph. n.d. "Why LINQ Beats SQL." LINQPad. http://www.linqpad.net/WhyLINQBeatsSQL.aspx.

Hasan, Nourul. 2012. "History of C# Programming." *All About C# Programming*, September 27. http://aboutcsharpprogramming.blogspot.com/2012/09/history-of-c-programming.html.

Know Your Meme. 2012. "Steve Ballmer Monkey Dance." http://knowyourmeme.com/memes/steve-ballmer-monkey-dance.

Landwerth, Immo. 2014. "NET Core Is Open Source." *.NET Blog*, November 12. http://blogs.msdn.com/b/dotnet/archive/2014/11/12/net-core-is-open-source.aspx.

Microsoft Developer Network. n.d. "LINQ (Language-Integrated Query)." https://msdn.microsoft.com/en-us/library/bb397926.aspx.

RECOMMENDED RESOURCES

Albahari, Joseph, and Ben Albahari. 2012. *C# 5.0 in a Nutshell: The Definitive Reference*. 5th ed. Sebastopol, CA: O'Reilly Media. This is a tightly packed reference book. Not to be read from start to finish, but in small spoonfuls like awful-tasting medicine, when and as needed.

Allen, Scott. 2014. "C# Fundamentals with C# 5.0." Pluralsight. http://www.pluralsight.com/courses/csharp-fundamentals-csharp5. A six-hour beginner's video course on C#. Scott Allen is a highly regarded voice in the .NET community. Find his blog, training courses, and podcasts at http://odetocode.com.

ASP.NET. n.d. "Get Started with ASP.NET." http://www.asp.net/get-started. Microsoft's introductory web page to ASP.NET. Not specific to C# but very helpful for understanding the bigger picture.

LINQPad. http://www.linqpad.net/.

Microsoft Developer Network. n.d. ".NET Framework Class Library." https://msdn.microsoft.com/en-us/library/gg145045(v=VS.110).aspx. The official documentation for all the classes in the .NET framework. Dry as bones but describes how each .NET class expects to be used, with terse examples. You'll visit often.

Visual Studio. https://www.visualstudio.com/.

Wikibooks. n.d. *C# Programming*. https://en.wikibooks.org/wiki/C_Sharp_Programming.

Chapter Ten

Java

Amanda Cowell

HISTORY AND DEVELOPMENT

Java is a class-based object-oriented programming language developed with the tagline "write once, run anywhere" (WORA), meaning that it is platform independent and its code can be compiled once and run on any platform. Other similar languages, such as C++, require a specific compiler for each platform. Java was also designed for simplicity and can automatically manage the creation and deletion of memory, which reduces coding errors. While Java is widely used for Internet applications, it was actually not created with online applications in mind. Java was initially created for embedded applications inside household electronics, such as microwave ovens and dishwashers. Many different brands of appliances need the same software capabilities but use different hardware. That is why platform independence became so important. As the web grew in popularity, it was discovered that Java's portability was ideal for online environments as well. Today, despite being an older language, Java has maintained its popularity and is the main platform used in developing applications for Android mobile devices.

Java, initially called Oak, was developed in 1991 by Sun Microsystems. It was created as part of something called the Green Project. The goal of Sun's Green Project was to create a portable programing language that could be run on multiple operating systems without having to recompile the code. At the time of Java's development, most large-scale computer programs were being developed in C++. C++ was based on C but added an object-oriented design that made it easier for programmers to manage and maintain large-scale projects. While C++ is a versatile language that can be run on nearly any platform, it requires a compiler for each type of hardware it is run on. A new solution was needed to create software that could be embedded in various consumer electronics, such as microwave ovens and telephones, regardless of the type of hardware used in those products (Schildt 2011). There were five primary goals for the development of the Java language:

- Simple, object oriented, and familiar
- Robust and secure
- Architecturally neutral and portable
- High performing
- Interpreted, threaded, and dynamic

Essentially, they wanted to create a programming language that was easy to use to develop large-scale programs that could run efficiently and on any platform (Oracle 1997).

Java was released to the public in 1995, around the same time that the Internet was growing in popularity. It soon became apparent that the same cross-platform issues plaguing embedded code would also be a problem for code developed to run on the Internet due to hardware, browser, and operating system incompatibility. Java naturally developed into the programming language most used for Internet applications (Schildt 2011).

In 1999, Sun Microsystems released Java 2 Platform Micro Edition (J2ME) as a platform for mobile phones and other similar devices. There was not a great deal of interest in consumer applications for these devices at the time, and mobile phone hardware was not ready to support these types of applications. As mobile phones and other mobile devices grew in popularity and the hardware capabilities of these devices improved, Java's ability to create content for these devices improved as well. In 2008, the first-generation Android phones were released and, by 2013, Android had 81.3 percent of the global smartphone market (Deitel, Deitel, and Deitel 2014). Java powers all of the applications running on all those devices, proving that despite its age, Java is still a powerful and important programming language.

USES

While Java code is portable to any similar application, the process of packaging a Java application for deployment is very different depending on what type of application you are creating (Gassner 2011). For example, you do not package a mobile application the same as a desktop application or a web application. In most cases, the executables will still be .jar files, but they will be created and run differently. This means that code written to power one type of microwave oven will run on another microwave oven with different hardware, but it is unlikely to run on a web browser, or, likewise, an android app is unlikely to run on a microwave oven. Applications are still portable from device to device of the same type, but write once, run anywhere doesn't quite mean what it used to.

Along the same lines, there are different tools required to develop different types of applications. For example, if you are planning on developing an application for Android, you will need to install the Android SDK/ADT Bundle to get access to the classes and tools needed to develop Android applications. You can download this bundle at http://developer.android.com/sdk/index .html. Different Java libraries and development environments do not make things more complicated but are needed so that developers can make use of features specific to the device they are developing for. For example, Android mobile devices have multitouch screens, and Java applications developed for those devices need to make use of various touch-screen gestures (Deitel, Deitel, and Deitel 2014).

If you are developing web-based applications in Java, it can be worthwhile to create a Java applet as opposed to a Java console-based application. A Java applet is a small application that can be embedded inside a web page. Applets are ideal for web applications as they have limited access to local resources, which avoids the spread of computer viruses and helps protect the privacy of users. In order to build an applet, the user needs to include the Abstract Window Toolkit (AWT) and the applet package, which contains the class `Applet`. Every applet created needs to be a subclass of `Applet` (Schildt 2011). Applets have decreased in popularity as other tools can frequently perform these same tasks more quickly and Java applets have faced some security issues in the past, but Java applets are still a powerful and frequently used tool on the web.

Due to Java's age, popularity, and open-source design, there are hundreds of tools, both free and paid, available to assist Java developers with any project. There are tools for Java development, such as integrated development environments (IDEs), which are discussed later in the chapter. Tools for debugging and testing code are widely available. There are tools to assist in developing graphics. In Java's twenty years of use, developers have tested and expanded its limits in every direction, and it is always worthwhile to look for a Java tool to assist with any project.

PROS AND CONS

Despite being an older language, Java is constantly evolving and has many current applications. It is simple, object oriented, architecturally neutral, and portable to nearly any platform. Java is the language used in native Android apps as well as for the creation of dynamic web applications. If you are looking to develop a mobile application for your library, learning Java is a necessity.

Java's age adds some benefits as well, as it has been well used and well documented over the last two decades. Tools have been developed for almost every task a Java beginner might want to undertake. There is also a large community of developers offering support to other users. It is not difficult to find online instructions or solutions to most problems encountered during development.

While scripting languages have gained popularity over the years, such as JavaScript (which is unrelated to Java), Perl, Python, and Ruby, to name a few, they are not well suited to large-scale programming. Scripting languages are popular because they use a structure that is easier to learn and allows for faster development of code. While many scripting languages are developing advancements that are increasing their capabilities, they are still significantly less usable for building large applications (Niemeyer and Leuck 2013).

Alternatively, despite its simplistic design, Java can be a complicated language to learn because it requires the developer to understand object-oriented programming. To really succeed as a Java developer, it is not enough to know Java syntax; it is also necessary to have a good understanding of objects, classes, and inheritance. This can make learning Java a larger undertaking than users initially expect. The good news about this is that Java makes this as simple as possible, and many IDEs can make development easier for beginners.

Also, while Java is a portable language for development, it can no longer be said that Java can run on any platform. Apple IOS does not allow Java to run on Apple devices such as iPhones and iPads. This requires non-Java versions of sites to be created for mobile usage since a great number of mobile users connect from Apple devices. Also, any mobile application developed in Java for Android devices needs to be recreated for the IOS environment. The impact of this on the popularity of the Java language is currently unknown, but it is clear that Java compatibility no longer has an impact on a product's usage or popularity. Without Java, web development will still go on.

ENVIRONMENT AND SETUP

The first step to Java development is to make sure Java is installed on your machine. Microsoft Windows machines already have Java installed, and Windows users can skip the remainder of this paragraph. If you are on a Mac, you may or may not have Java installed on your machine, depending on what operating system you are using. The best way to test if you are running Java on your Mac is to open up Terminal and type `java -version`. You may get an error that you don't have Java or you may see a number string that indicates your Java version. For example, if terminal outputs Java version 1.8.0_45, you are running Java 8 on your machine. If you find that you do not have Java or you have an outdated version, go here for instructions on how to download the latest version of Java onto your machine: https://www .java.com/en/download/help/mac_install.xml.

The next step for both Mac and Windows users is to install the Java Development Kit (JDK). JDK is the most widely used software development kit (SDK) for Java development, and it is offered for free from Oracle. As of the writing of this book, the most recent version of JDK for Java SE (Standard Edition) can be found here: http://www.oracle.com/technetwork/java/javase/ downloads/index.html. Downloading JDK will install everything needed to develop in Java, including the Java Virtual Machine.

Once installed, Java is ready to go, but before you start programming, you need to choose a text editor. While Java software files are just text files and can be edited in any text editing software, there are a lot of options to choose from. If you are already a seasoned programmer, you can continue using text editing tools you have used in the past. Alternatively, IDEs are very useful when starting out, especially if you are somewhat new to software development, as they can help you build, edit, debug, and compile your applications.

There are many IDE options that are great for getting started. Some IDEs only run on Macs, some only run on Windows, and many are cross-platform. There are free IDEs and also paid ones that offer more complex functions for a licensing fee. Some IDEs work well for small-scale programs while others are better for larger, more involved projects. There are many factors to consider and many pros and cons of each tool.

One good IDE to start with is Eclipse. Eclipse is not necessarily the right environment for everyone, but there many advantages to Eclipse. Eclipse can be used on Windows or Mac, is open source and free to use, and has Android developer tools built in, which can make it a great tool for beginner Android developers. It is also the tool that was used to develop the example code in this chapter. To install Eclipse, go to http://www.eclipse.org/down loads. You will see a number of distributions of Eclipse; you want to choose "Eclipse IDE for Java Developers."

EXAMPLES

Hello World

This is a basic Hello World application. It is a good way to test your Java runtime environment to make sure you can successfully compile and run code.

```
public class HelloWorld
{

     public static void main(String[] args)
     {
          System.out.println("Hello World!!!!");
     }
}
```

If run successfully, this code will simply print out the line `Hello World!!!!` Despite its simplicity, it is worth taking a look at this code line by line to better understand what it is doing.

```
public class HelloWorld {
```

The first line is creating a class called `Hello World`. Every Java application is built inside a class. This makes it very different from other programming environments. In Java, everything is an object, and an object is created from a class. Inside classes, code is wrapped in functions.

```
public static void main(String[] args)
```

The function above in the simple Hello World program is called `main` because it is where our main code is executed. There is only one main function in any application, and it must always be declared `public static void` and accept a `String`, which is traditionally named `args`. This function is called automatically by the Java Virtual Machine, and your code will not work without it.

```
System.out.println("Hello World!!!!");
```

The last line of the code is the code that prints out the text we want.

Expanded Hello World

The program below produces the exact same output as the program above. In order to explain further what is meant by saying everything is an object, a second class has been created called `Welcomer`.

```
public class HelloWorld
{
     public static void main(String[] args)
     {
          Welcomer welcomer = new Welcomer();
```

```
            welcomer.sayHello();
    }
}
public class Welcomer
{
        private String welcome = "Hello World!!!!";
        public void sayHello()
        {
            System.out.println(welcome);
        }
}
```

The initial class `Hello World` still exists and still contains the mandatory main function that Java needs to run.

```
public class HelloWorld {
public static void main(String[] args) {
```

The first thing the main function does is create a `Welcomer`.

```
Welcomer welcomer = new Welcomer();
```

A `Welcomer` for the purposes of this program can be thought of as an object that shouts "Hello World!!!!" when told to say hello. You can imagine that you have created an actual physical object, such as a tiny robot, that can perform tasks. Now we just need to tell it to say hello.

```
welcomer.sayHello();
```

In order for this to work though, a second class `Welcomer` needs to be defined.

```
public class Welcomer {
```

This class is what creates our welcome and contains all of the welcome attributes. Every function the welcome can perform is inside this class. Inside this class, we create a string with our hello text.

```
private String welcome = "Hello World!!!!";
```

Then we create a new function that prints out our string of hello text.

```
public void sayHello() {
System.out.println(welcome);
}
}
```

This code obviously made a very simple function, printing out `Hello World!!!!`, significantly more complicated. It was mostly done to show how everything in Java is an object. There are many reasons you want to create classes with different behaviors. Creating multiple classes is still a useful practice as it simplifies the process of expanding your programs. For example, if the programmer decided to add tasks to the `Welcomer`, such as asking the user of the program to fill out an introductory survey, new code could be added by creating new functions inside the `Welcomer` class and called from the main function with limited modification to existing code.

More Than One Right Way

In Java, as in many other programming languages, there are often multiple ways to complete the same class. One way is not necessarily better than the other. Sometimes the choice depends on how the code is being used. In other cases, it can come down to the preference of the developer. The example below shows four different methods of looping over a simple array. Each type of loop produces the same output.

```
public class Main {
static private String[] numbers = {"one", "two", "three",
"four", "five"};
     public static void main(String[] args)
     {
     for (String number : numbers) //for each loop
     {
          System.out.println(number);
     }
     for (int number=0; number < numbers.length; number++)
     //for loop
     {
          System.out.println(numbers[number]);
     }
     int number = 0;
     while(number < numbers.length) //while loop
     {
          System.out.println(numbers[number]);
          number++;
     }
     number = 0;
     do //do while loop
     {
          System.out.println(numbers[number]);
          number++;
     } while (number < numbers.length);
}
}
```

The loops used above are for, for each, while, and do while, as shown by the comments. None of these choices is wrong or right, and none works more or less efficiently than another. Many times in Java there will be choices about how to execute a program, and it is possible that five experienced programmers would come up with five different solutions and all of them would be correct. While developing in Java, or any programming language, it is important for a developer to have an open mind, be creative, and find a style that suits him or her. This is not to say there aren't right and wrong choices in many circumstance, but there is a lot of room for creativity and personal style as well.

Using Built-In Classes

One of the great things about Java is there are a lot of built-in classes that already contain functions to do tasks you may want to do. Before writing a program in Java, it is often worthwhile to see if there is already a Java class that can do the operations you want to do. Here is an example that uses calendar classes built into Java. The program below reads in the month, day, and year of your birth and returns the day of the week that you were born. For example, if you were born on July 25, 1977, the program would return the word Monday, as that particular date fell on a Monday.

```
import java.util.Calendar;
import java.util.GregorianCalendar;
import java.util.Scanner;
public class Main
{
    public static void main(String[] args)
    {
        Scanner input = new Scanner( System.in);
        System.out.println("Enter the month of your
        birth");
        int month = input.nextInt(); //Read in birth
        month
        System.out.println("Enter the day of your
        birth");
        int day = input.nextInt(); //Read in birth day
        System.out.println("Enter the year of your
        birth");
        int year = input.nextInt(); //Read in birth year
        month = month-1; //Months in Java are 0-11
        instead of 1-12
        GregorianCalendar birthday = new
        GregorianCalendar(year, month, day);
```

```
String namesOfDays[] = { "Sunday", "Monday",
"Tuesday", "Wednesday", "Thursday", "Friday",
"Saturday"};
String weekday = namesOfDays[(birthday.
get(Calendar.DAY_OF_WEEK)) - 1];
System.out.println(weekday);
input.close();
    }
}
```

This program imports three existing Java classes:

```
import java.util.Calendar;
import java.util.GregorianCalendar;
import java.util.Scanner;
```

The class `java.util.Calendar` is an abstract class that provides methods for converting between a specific instant in time and a set of calendar fields such as YEAR, MONTH, and so on, and for manipulating the calendar fields, such as getting the date of the next week. An instant in time can be represented by a millisecond value that is an offset from the Epoch, January 1, 1970, 00:00:00.000 GMT (Gregorian) (Oracle 2015).

The `java.util.GregorianCalendar` is a concrete subclass of `Calendar` and provides the standard calendar system used by most of the world. The GregorianCalendar class allows the programmer to enter a date in a familiar format (month, date, year, etc.) and easily convert it to a date that Java understands. The GregorianCalendar class also allows for math functions so you can manipulate dates by adding and subtracting time from them (Oracle 2015). The class `java.util.Scanner` is one of many ways that data can be read into Java. It is a simple text scanner that can parse primitive types and strings using regular expressions (Oracle 2015).

One important thing to remember when using an existing Java class is that it may not work exactly the way you expect. It is important to understand the functions of a class before you use them, or you may get undesirable results. For example, after the code above reads in an integer for the month, it subtracts one.

```
month = month-1; //Months in the Calendar class are 0-11
instead of 1-12
GregorianCalendar birthday = new GregorianCalendar(year,
month, day);
```

This is because, as the comment indicates, months in the calendar class go from 0 to 11 instead of 1 to 12. If a user of this program was born in January, he or she would likely enter 1 for the birth month when prompted, but Java would interpret that to mean February. It is the responsibility of the program developer to make sure that the data is being interpreted properly.

This specific example may never come up, but there will be a lot of times that a class or function doesn't behave in exactly the way an unfamiliar user might expect. It is always a good idea to read through the documentation when using something new.

There are many of these types of built-in classes that help with various operations, such as File (java.io.File), which allows users to edit files; Math (java.io.Math) for complex math equations; or NumberFormat (java.io.NumberFormat), which allows users to specify their number format down to details such as currency type, including euros verses American dollars. A list of all classes included with Java 8 can be found here: http://docs.oracle.com/javase/8/docs/api/allclasses-noframe.html.

If you want to see what methods are included in a class or how to use a particular method, it is worthwhile to look up the documentation on that class. Also, if you try to use something and it doesn't work the way you expect, it is always useful to search Java forums on the Internet. It is very likely that someone had the same confusion as you.

Java Applet

This is an example of code that will generate a Java applet that can be embedded in a web browser. Unlike console-based applications, code for applets does not require a static void main function to run. This function uses the graphic class very minimally, but it can be used to do more complex drawings. There is also a 3D graphics class that allows for three-dimensional graphics and many other graphics classes as well.

All this application does is create a box containing words in red that say "This is a Java Applet."

```
import java.applet.Applet;
import java.awt.Graphics;
import java.awt.Color;
public class Main extends Applet
{
    public void paint(Graphics g) {
    Color color = Color.RED;
    g.setColor(color);
    g.drawString("This is a Java Applet", 25, 25);
    }
}
```

This uses the Color class to set the color of the text. In this case, the example uses a built-in constant of RED, but the code would also allow a color hex code to get the exact color the user wants.

SUMMARY

Java is a robust, portable, object-oriented, and familiar language. It is the language used in all Android applications and can also be used for many other types of projects, including everything from developing web applications to programming SIM cards and other microdevices. While Java can be more complicated to learn than some newer languages, it is a mature language with a strong history, large user base, and vast tool set available to help both new and veteran users. Java's portability, usability, and maturity make it a powerful tool for a wide variety of large and small programming projects.

BIBLIOGRAPHY

Deitel, P., H. Deitel, and A. Deitel. 2014. *Android for Programmers: An App-Driven Approach.* Upper Saddle River, NJ: Prentice Hall.
Gassner, D. 2011. "Java Essential Training." Lynda.com. http://www.lynda.com/Java-tutorials/Java-Essential-Training/377484-2.html.
Murach, J. 2011. *Java Programming.* 4th ed. Fresno, CA: Mike Murach & Associates.
Niemeyer, P., and D. Leuck. 2013. *Learning Java.* Beijing: O'Reilly Media.
Oh, H. S., B. J. Kim, H. K. Choi, and S. M. Moon. 2012. "Evaluation of Android Dalvik Virtual Machine." In *Proceedings of the 10th International Workshop on Java Technologies for Real-Time and Embedded Systems*, 115–24. New York: ACM.
Oracle. 1997. "Design Goals of the Java Programming Language." *The Java Programming Language Environment.* http://www.oracle.com/technetwork/java/intro-141325.html.
———. 2015. "Java Platform, Standard Edition 8 API Specification." http://docs.oracle.com/javase/8/docs/api/overview-summary.html.
Schildt, H. 2011. *Java the Complete Reference: Comprehensive Coverage of the Java Language.* 8th ed. New York: McGraw-Hill.
Schildt, H., and J. Holmes. 2003. *The Art of Java.* New York: McGraw-Hill.

RECOMMENDED RESOURCES

Java Essential Training Online Course. http://www.lynda.com/Java-tutorials/Java-Essential-Training/377484-2.html (requires subscription).
Oracle's site where Java, Java tools, and documentation can be found: http://www.oracle.com/technetwork/java/index.html.
Schildt, H. 2014. *Java: A Beginner's Guide.* New York: McGraw-Hill Education.
Stack Overflow. http://stackoverflow.com/. This is a site of user-generated questions and answers and is a great place to find someone who is doing or has done the same thing you are trying to do. Like most collaborative online sites, not all of the information is correct, and content is not mediated for quality.

Glossary

Eric Phetteplace, Amanda Cowell, and Beth Thomsett-Scott

Important note: Many terms have different meanings depending on the language they are used in as well as the stage of programming. For convenience, we have defined some of the most important terms below. A few web resources are presented at the end for further assistance. There are also a variety of dictionaries and handbooks in print or online that will be helpful for beginners.

AJAX. An acronym for Asynchronous JavaScript and XML, AJAX is a technique for dynamically pulling in data from other websites or services without requiring the web browser to refresh the page. AJAX is an important and common technique in modern web development because of how it makes websites feel faster and allows multiple data sources to be combined by a web app in real time.

applet. A small program that can be sent along with a web page to a user.

array. An object that holds a set number of values of one type. Values are usually in columns and rows.

asynchronous programming. A form of programming that allows different activities (events) to occur before a previous one is completed. For example, you are shutting off your computer—asynchronous programming allows each program to close and exit without following an order. Synchronous programming would request Word to exit before starting to close Excel.

class-based programming. A style of object-oriented programming in which inheritance is achieved by defining classes of objects, as opposed to the objects themselves.

compiler/compiled language. A computer program (or set of programs) that accepts source code and produces a binary executable; in other words, it is another program that executes the instructions contained within the code. A compiled programming language is a language that is sent through a compiler first before any code is executed. Compare with *interpreter/ interpreted language.*

console-based application. A computer program designed to be used via a text-only computer interface.

database structure. The database structure defines the format for organizing and storing data. There are a variety of different structure types, but most will specify the file, array, record, and table. Types of structures include flat files (records within do not have any relationship among them), relational (multiple databases that have a relationship with each other), and object oriented (data are treated as objects).

data type. A data type is an attribute that specifies the type of data an object is able to hold. This data-type specification affects the values, operations, the way values can be stored, and the meaning of the data. Data types include text, byte, integer, currency, and many more.

declarative language. A term used to describe high-level programming languages that, without the programmer knowing an exact procedure, can be used to solve problems.

embedded application. A software application that permanently resides in an industrial or consumer device.

environment. In general, the programming environment is the base on which the programming is performed. This includes the software and hardware needed to complete the programming function.

filehandle (file handle). A number that an operating system assigns to a file immediately after it is opened.

function. In the context of programming languages, a function is a construct that takes an input, performs some operations, and then possibly returns an output value. Unlike mathematical functions, programming functions can operate on nonnumeric input. For instance, a `toUppercase` function might take a string of text and return the same text but with all lowercase letters transformed into their uppercase equivalent.

gem. A gem is a self-contained holder for Ruby programs and libraries. RubyGems is a packaging manager that is used to distribute the gems.

hash. Hashes are similar to arrays, but rather than requiring values to be integers, hashes allow any object type.

HTML. An acronym for HyperText Markup Language, the markup language that powers the web. HTML features angle-bracket-encased "tags" like `<title>` that tell web browsers what the meaning and function of different text strings should be.

HTML5. A loose group of web browser features and standards that aimed to move the World Wide Web from static documents to a full-fledged application development platform that could compete with mobile and desktop operating systems. Examples of HTML5 features include geolocation, client-side data storage, and the `<video>` and `<audio>` HTML tags.

inheritance. When an object or class is based on another object or class, using the same implementation to maintain the same behavior.

integrated development environment (IDE). A software application that provides comprehensive facilities to computer programmers for software development. An IDE normally consists of a source-code editor, build automation tools, and a debugger.

interpreter/interpreted language. A computer program that accepts source code and immediately executes its instructions without creating another executable program in the interim. An interpreted programming language is a language that uses an interpreter to execute its code. Compare with *compiler/compiled language.*

library. In computer programming, a library is a collection of similar objects stored for infrequent use, often to develop software. These may include configuration data, documentation, help data, message templates, prewritten code and subroutines, classes, values, or type specifications.

loop. A loop is a repeated sequence of coded instructions. The sequence is repeated until a specified condition is met.

object/object-oriented programming (OOP). A programming language that combines data structures with functions to create reusable objects. These objects have data fields (attributes that describe the object) and associated procedures known as methods. For instance, in a program a `book` object might have both a `title` property that is a text string as well as a `get_cover_image` method that, when invoked, returns a cover image pulled from a third-party service. Most programming languages support some form of OOP.

parse. Parsing text or code means to separate the string of text (think of it as a sentence in literature) into its component parts.

portable. The usability of the same software in different environments.

private variable. A variable that is visible only to the class to which it belongs.

procedural programming. Procedural languages are those that function in a step-by-step process, establishing each procedure that needs to be completed before moving on to the next. Generally, these are older languages, such as C.

protected variable. A variable that is visible only to the class to which it belongs and any subclasses.

public variable. A variable that is visible to all classes.

regex. Regex (regular expression) is a string or sequence of text or code that is used to describe a search pattern. Regexes are useful for searching code to find a particular sequence or pattern to update or modify.

runtime environment. Runtime environment is essentially the configuration of software and hardware needed to support the program. Environment support includes CPU type, operating system, and other programs or add-ons needed to perform the tasks.

script. Scripts are sequences of instructions or programs that are read and carried out by another program rather than the computer itself or a human operator. This enhances the automation of the function(s) being performed.

scripting language. A scripting language supports the use of scripts.

software development kit (SDK). A set of software development tools that allows the creation of applications for a certain software package.

strongly or weakly typed language. These terms are often subjective depending on the point of view of the individual. However, in general, a strongly typed language is one needing each variable or value to be assigned a data type. A weakly typed language is more flexible in that data types do not need to be explicitly assigned.

terminal. A terminal allows you to communicate with a computer or web page. Communication is bidirectional—sending and receiving information. Usually, a terminal involves a display screen and keyboard, although there are more sophisticated terminals.

type/type system. A programming language with a type system that internally associates each data structure with one of an enumerated set of types—which often can be added to by the programmer—that each have distinct behaviors and can perhaps only be involved in certain kinds of operations. For instance, it is a type system that would insist that a text string `hello` could not be multiplied by the floating-point number `1.23`.

XHR/XmlHttpRequest. See *AJAX.*

Here are a few websites that may help you as you read through the text:

http://www.computerhope.com/jargon.htm
http://www.math.utah.edu/~wisnia/glossary.html
http://www.csci.csusb.edu/dick/cs202/glossary.html
http://www.cs.kent.ac.uk/people/staff/djb/oop/glossary.html
http://whatis.techtarget.com/glossary/Programming

Additional Resources

Editor's note: It was difficult selecting items since there are many to choose from, as well as a bevy of online options. The items below come from personal experience, examining reviews with many grains of salt, and recommendations from colleagues who code. There are others, frequently the For Dummies, O'Reilly, and Head Start items, which may work as well. Videos, including those on YouTube, offer great tips and programming examples, as do online forums and training sites. As librarians, however, we all know to evaluate the quality of our sources.

GENERAL RESOURCES

Codecademy: http://codeacademy.com. Free interactive, although text-based, courses to learn the fundamentals of Python, Ruby, JavaScript, PHP, SQL, and Java.

Code School: https://www.codeschool.com/free. Free courses for learning the basics of Ruby, JavaScript, and SQL.

Coding Bat: http://codingbat.com/. Coding practice for Java and Python. Not so much a tutorial as a place to see examples and determine the logic behind them. Text and video instruction. Good source once you understand how it is designed.

W3Schools: http://www.w3schools.com/. Free tutorials and code examples for JavaScript, SQL, and PHP.

BOOKS

General Programming and Coding

Abraham, Nikhil. 2015. *Coding For Dummies*. New York: For Dummies. Focused on the web-based languages (JavaScript, Ruby, and Python), this book helps readers understand interactions among languages as they work together and the features of

171

each. Readers will build an actual web-based application. Includes inspecting code through a browser tool. Requires basic terminology knowledge but does explain beginning topics well. An environment for trying out tutorials and practice coding and receiving output is provided, and "End of Chapter" challenges are included. Online exercises developed by Codecademy to help hone coding skills and demonstrate results as you practice.

Farrell, Mary E. 2007. *Computer Programming for Teens*. Boston: Cengage Learning. Recommended for the effective explanation of concepts and basic programming topics. Having a solid background and understanding of concepts and terminology will makes it easier to learn the syntax of programming languages.

Martin, Robert C. 2008. *Clean Code: A Handbook of Agile Software Craftsmanship*. Upper Saddle River, NJ: Prentice Hall. Presents best practices for coding, including items such as meaningful names, pertinent comments, formatting for followers, and more. Java is the language used in the examples, but guidelines are applicable across most languages. Recommended to read early to follow best practices.

Sande, Warren, and Carter Sande. 2013. *Hello World! Computer Programming for Kids and Other Beginners*. 2nd ed. Greenwich, CT: Manning. Not just for kids. Easy-to-follow instructions. Although written for early teens, the images, analogies, and language let readers focus on content rather than complicated terminology. Brings complex ideas, such as variable nested loops, into layperson terms. Authors do not assume even a basic level of technical knowledge. Helpful features are notes and an appendix that provide some key differences between Python 2.x and Python 3.x. Offers exercises at ends of chapters. Software is easy to install and access. Includes focus on game development. Provides "Test Your Knowledge" and "Try It Out" sections.

Wang, Wallace. 2008. *Beginning Programming All-in-One Desk Reference for Dummies*. New York: For Dummies. Good overview of computer science but does not teach programming per se. It does offer programming basics in a number of languages. Examples will not work due to age of book. Discusses important concepts, including compiling, algorithms, debugging, best practices, and much more. Advanced concepts include bioinformatics, computer security, and artificial intelligence.

Yelton, Andromeda. 2015. *Coding for Librarians: Learning by Example*. Chicago: American Library Association. Compiles interviews with librarians to gather examples of real-life learnable programs that are in libraries today, thanks to librarians who learned to code to solve problems.

Zelle, John. 2010. *Python Programming: An Introduction to Computer Science*. 2nd ed. Portland, OR: Franklin, Beedle & Associates. Very good introduction to theoretical computer science concepts in general, with a focus on problem solving with Python 3 as language of choice. Reviewed as being an excellent item for beginners, both to programming in general and Python specifically. Examples are somewhat mathematically based so can be harder to learn but do provide solid examples of what can be accomplished. Does not teach Python step by step. Other books provide better Python programming.

Python

Severance, Charles R. 2013. *Python for Informatics: Exploring Information.* Seattle: CreateSpace. Free and best used in conjunction with his Coursera (coursera.com) course. Despite the title, it is an introduction to Python with real-world data examples as the backdrop. A good starter book written in a concise yet engaging style. Works with Python 2.x.

Shaw, Zed A. 2015. *Learn Python the Hard Way.* http://learnpythonthehardway.org/book/. Solid overview of Python for beginners. Not always the easiest to follow but does provide a comprehensive tutorial style.

Sweigart, Al. 2015. *Automate the Boring Stuff with Python: Practical Programming for Total Beginners.* San Francisco: No Starch Press. Skills and concepts for those new to Python programming, but not necessarily the absolute beginner. Provides solid background to programming concepts in general. Breaks content into bit-sized chunks for retention. Build tools that have everyday use so readers gain real-world applications. Covers Python 3.x.

Ruby

Metz, Sandi. 2012. *Practical Object-Oriented Design in Ruby: An Agile Primer.* Boston: Addison-Wesley. A solid treatise in object-oriented design. Uses Ruby as the backdrop, but content is extendable to other object-oriented languages. Might be too much for absolute beginners but well worth the read once you have the underpinnings of Ruby.

Pine, Chris. *Learn to Program.* 2nd ed. Frisco, TX: Pragmatic Bookshelf. A good introduction to programming with Ruby. Later chapters introduce more advanced concepts and may be too much for beginners, so be wary. Exercises with answers, including both basic answers and "enhanced" answers.

JavaScript

Free Code Camp. http://www.freecodecamp.com/. Free online source for practicing JavaScript.

Myers, Mark. 2014. *A Smarter Way to Learn JavaScript: The New Approach That Uses Technology to Cut Your Effort in Half.* Seattle: CreateSpace. Provides a solid foundation for JavaScript fundamentals, especially the very basic things that a lot of "beginner" books neglect. Written in easy-to-follow language and with a well-thought-out design. Provides a sandbox environment to practice the examples in. Strongly interactive. Vast array of examples.

Zakas, Nicholas C. 2014. *The Principles of Object-Oriented JavaScript.* San Francisco: No Starch Press. Builds on some basics as it works solely with JavaScript's object-oriented nature. Very clear explanations.

Perl

Christiansen, Tom, Brian D. Foy, Larry Wall, and Jon Orwant. 2012. *Programming Perl: Unmatched Power for Text Processing and Scripting*. 4th ed. Sebastopol, CA: O'Reilly Media. Considered to be *the* book on Perl. Not known as a beginner's book but a second tier once you have some programming experience.
Schwartz, Randal L., Brian D. Foy, and Tom Phoenix. 2011. *Learning Perl*. 6th ed. Sebastopol, CA: O'Reilly Media. Offers a very practical approach to the mechanics of Perl, focusing on cumulative knowledge as the chapters move along. Excellent introduction to learning Perl. May need to have a book on general programming nearby, as this does not introduce programming concepts per se.

PHP

C4Learn.com. http://www.c4learn.com/php/php-syntax/. Well-designed site with table of contents always visible on left side. Leads the user through the basics to more complicated programming with easy-to-follow examples.
PHP The Right Way. http://www.phptherightway.com/. Covers a multitude of basics through advanced information, including templates, errors and exceptions, servers and deployment, and additional resources.

SQL

Forta, Ben. 2012. *SQL in 10 Minutes*. 4th ed. Indianapolis: Sams. Provides solid background for beginners to use SQL. Most-common statements and clauses. Defines terms well. Introduces some advanced topics at the end to show what SQL can do. Teaches by example using the major DBMSs: MYSQL, SQL Server, Oracle, and DB2. The downloadable material along with the step-by-step instructions, and the two free database utilities, help cement the information.

C

Perry, Greg, and Dean Miller. 2013. *C Programming Absolute Beginner's Guide*. 3rd ed. Indianapolis: Que. This is a great book for beginners that starts from the basics and leads the user into more advanced topics. The authors have broken the topics into short chapters that provide strong and diverse examples. Content is written for nontechies.

C#

Miles, Rob. 2015. *The C# Programming Yellow Book*. http://www.robmiles.com/c-yellow-book/. Also available as an Amazon Kindle ebook. Provides specifics regarding the C# language and offers a good background in recommended practices for professional programming. Well written and easy to follow.

Using the Visual C# Development Environment. https://msdn.microsoft.com/en-us/library/ms173063.aspx. Good coverage of the interplay between Visual Studio 2015 and C#.

Java

Eck, David J. *Introduction to Programming Using Java*. 7th ed. http://math.hws.edu/javanotes/. Freely available, regularly updated. Developed exclusively for beginners. Provides a decent overview of programming concepts as well as an introduction to programming in Java.

Sedgewick, Robert, and Kevin Wayne. 2007. *Introduction to Programming in Java: An Interdisciplinary Approach*. New York: Pearson. Very well-designed book aimed at beginners. Includes solid explanations of programming terms and concepts. Coding examples are practical and illustrate a particular point or technique to solidify the text.

Index

About the Editor and Contributors

Beth Thomsett-Scott has nearly twenty years of experience as a science librarian and currently serves as the engineering librarian at the University of North Texas (UNT). She has been with UNT since 2001, when she relocated from Canada. She is passionate about providing library users with the ability to find, access, and utilize the information they need. Her research interests include website usability, user needs and satisfaction studies, and coaching/ mentoring library employees. Thomsett-Scott has served extensively with the Science and Technology Section of the American Library Association, the Texas Library Association, and several other regional and national organizations, including serving as a chair of divisions/sections and as a secretary and chairing a variety of committees. Her current service focus is the Engineering and Sci-Tech Divisions of the Special Libraries Association, where she serves in several roles. She has edited two books and has a variety of publication and presentation credits.

Jason Bengtson is the innovation architect at the Texas Medical Center Library in Houston, Texas. He holds an MLIS and MA from the University of Iowa and the University of New Mexico, respectively. He has held a number of technology-focused library positions, including emerging technologies/ R&D librarian for the University of New Mexico Health Sciences Library and Informatics Center and head of Library Computing and Information Systems at the University of Oklahoma's Robert M. Bird Library. He has published on a number of diverse topics, including a theoretical model to apply concepts of complexity science to metadata. Bengtson has built extensively with a wide assortment of languages and frameworks, including JavaScript, jQuery, jQuery UI, Bootstrap, AngularJS, HTML5, CSS3, PHP, XSLT, MySQL, ColdFusion, and Python.

Ashley Blewer is a web developer and archivist. She holds an MLIS as well as a bachelor's of art in graphic design from the University of South Carolina. She is a graduate of the Flatiron School's Web Immersive program and works as an independent consultant for digital archives and access to archival material, with an emphasis on audiovisual formats. She has previously worked in the private sector as an integrations engineer and at the University of South Carolina Moving Image Research Collections as a cataloging manager. She is a contributor to Bay Area Video Coalition's QC Tools, an open-source video quality-control software, and PREFORMA's video file conformance checker project, MediaConch.

Amanda Cowell is the emerging technologies librarian at the College of New Jersey. She has a BS in computer science from Stevens Institution of Technology and an MLIS and MBA from Rutgers University. Cowell previously worked as the technical lead for the Brooklyn Visual Heritage Project at the Brooklyn Public Library and as a digital archivist at Rutgers University. Prior to becoming a librarian, she worked for several years as a software design and development engineer for Lockheed Martin.

Heidi Frank is the electronic resources and special formats cataloging librarian at New York University. She has been a cataloger for more than fifteen years, primarily working in traditional technical services departments using the leading cataloging standards—MARC, AACR2, and LCSH. Over the past three years, Python scripting has become her primary tool for working with MARC data in order to improve quality control, batch processes, and create more efficient workflows, often through automation. She has published and presented on PyMARC and Python as tools for cataloging. She also serves on relevant professional committees.

Charles Ed Hill is the systems and digital services librarian at Westfield State University in Westfield, Massachusetts. Since finishing his MLS at Indiana University in 2012, Hill has spent many hours figuring out how to save a few minutes with code and enhancing user experience and accessibility one navigation bar at a time. He is current exploring Python for tool building and fun, as well as JavaScript and PHP.

Lauren Magnuson serves as the systems and emerging technologies librarian at California State University, Northridge. She has an MA in information science and a MEd in educational technology, both from the University of Missouri, as well as a BA in philosophy from Tulane University. Her interests include PHP, Python, analytics, and data visualization, as well as promoting open-source technology in academic libraries.

Emily R. Mitchell has an MLS from Indiana University and an MA in educational technology from Central Michigan University. She is currently the webmaster librarian at SUNY Oswego's Penfield Library and has worked previously as a programmer for Marick Learning and as a librarian at Ferris State University. Her research focuses on user experience on library websites.

Eric Phetteplace is systems librarian at California College of the Arts, where his primary duties are maintaining and developing websites, an institutional repository, and an ILS. Previously, he was emerging technologies librarian at Chesapeake College. He holds a bachelor's of arts and sciences in English and mathematics from Stanford University and an MLIS from the University of Illinois at Urbana-Champaign. In 2015, he was a fellow at the inaugural Institute of Open Leadership organized by Creative Commons. In his spare time, he plays the card game Netrunner and fiddles with code on GitHub.

Tim Ribaric has been the digital services librarian at Brock University since 2006. In addition to an MLIS, he has an undergraduate degree in computer science and is currently completing his master's of computer science. Most of his work is done in Python, but he has a soft spot for C, the language he cut his teeth on.

Jessica Rudder is a developer at the Flatiron School, where she focuses on building web applications that support adults and high school students in their efforts to learn to program in Ruby and Objective-C. She is a graduate of Flatiron School's Web Immersive program. In addition to her technical training, she holds a bachelor's of fine arts from New York University's Tisch School of the Arts. She has worked in digital marketing with brands, including Disney and major European yellow pages in Belgium, Portugal, and Sweden.

Jason Steelman holds a BA in media arts from USC and currently works for Robert Half Technology as a consultant in Des Moines, Iowa. He is a developer and technology leader in corporate, academic, and nonprofit institutions. His library experience includes work for the University of South Carolina with the William Gilmore Simms Initiatives, Moving Image Research Collections, Thomas Cooper Library, and Ernest F. Hollings Special Collections Library. Recent leadership includes USC's Interactive Media-Rich Educational Environment program, where he served as the project's lead.

Peter Tyrrell is the director and lead developer for Andornot Consulting in Vancouver, British Columbia (http://andornot.com). He graduated with a BA in classics and English literature from the University of Victoria in 1998 and an MLIS degree from the University of British Columbia in 2003. He was hired by Andornot in 2001, becoming a shareholding director in 2010. He enjoys programming and considers figuring out how to make things work to be the most fun. Tyrrell considers himself lucky to be paid to fix things. He's consulted for a variety of libraries, archives, and museums and codes on most days, usually in .NET and C#.

Dean Walton is the science and technology outreach librarian at the University of Oregon. He is the subject specialist for biology, geology, and environmental studies and is working on experiential learning programs as they relate to the library and his subject areas. His other interests include work on disaster informatics, ecological mapping, and environmental sensor systems. He has a Ph.D. in biological sciences and is a past vegetation ecologist for the Nature Conservancy and the Virginia and West Virginia Natural Heritage Programs.

Roy Zimmer works for the Library Systems Office at Western Michigan University. He has worked with NOTIS, Voyager, and now Alma+Primo library systems. He has written a number of MARC utilities available for anyone to use. He developed a normalization routine for good call number sorting. While the library was using Voyager, he implemented a number of vendor record data loads and also wrote the extracts to feed MeLCat (Michigan eLibrary Catalog), a statewide interlibrary loan partnership. He subsequently adapted these extracts for discovery services the library was using: the open-source VuFind and the commercial product Summon. He has presented at a number of annual user group meetings.